T0162710

SOCIAL JUSTICE

and

INTELLECTUAL SUPPRESSION

SOCIAL JUSTICE
and
INTELLECTUAL SUPPRESSION

TAYSIR NASHIF

authorHOUSE®

AuthorHouse™
1663 Liberty Drive
Bloomington, IN 47403
www.authorhouse.com
Phone: 1-800-839-8640

© 2011 by Taysir Nashif. All rights reserved.

No part of this book may be reproduced, stored in a retrieval system, or transmitted by any means without the written permission of the author.

First published by AuthorHouse   08/03/2011

ISBN: 978-1-4634-4459-4 (sc)
ISBN: 978-1-4634-4458-7 (ebk)

Printed in the United States of America

Any people depicted in stock imagery provided by Thinkstock are models, and such images are being used for illustrative purposes only.
Certain stock imagery © Thinkstock.

This book is printed on acid-free paper.

Because of the dynamic nature of the Internet, any web addresses or links contained in this book may have changed since publication and may no longer be valid. The views expressed in this work are solely those of the author and do not necessarily reflect the views of the publisher, and the publisher hereby disclaims any responsibility for them.

Contents

In memory of
Najm Al-Diin and
'Aa'isha Al-Nashif

Preface

The developing countries—including their peoples, societies and institutions—are heavily exposed to foreign cultural messages, which are transmitted by traditional and modern tools of technological communication media. Developing peoples, that are facing fateful social and economic challenges, are going through cultural, political and economic transitional stage. The fact that these peoples are going through this stage makes it easier for foreign cultural messages to exert a stronger influence in many walks of life. Attempts among the developing peoples to counter some foreign influences have made governmental and non-governmental bodies engaged for a long time, hence making it easier for such transmission of messages to be more effective.

The essential ideas in this book, which I have written in the last three years, are that politics, or the art of acquiring the means of influence to achieve goals, are inherent in all human relations; that thought is split between the interacting subjective and objective variable factors and is constrained by interactive social relations; that intellectual conservatism cannot catch up with dynamic intellectual reality; that ideology restrains intellectual emancipation, and that on the basis of dynamic interaction among natural, social, cultural, political and psychological variable factors, and of the preponderant role being played by the political factor, the adopted view is that political and social relations among individuals, groups, states, and other entities involve social and intellectual injustice.

In putting forth and analyzing these relations, the book pays a considerable attention to the developing countries. No understanding of the nature of the socio-cultural relations would be achieved without fathoming and grasping the political factor which is always present in such relations.

Factors, throughout the study, are understood as interrelated, dynamic and experiencing interaction.

Concepts, such as development, progress and awakening, or some of their aspects, are sometimes used interchangeably.

People's achievement of perfection is illusion. Because of their psychological conditions and their cultural, social, political and economic circumstances, they cannot reach perfection. Such circumstances prevent their attainment of perfection.

Suppression is one of the main topics in this book. Suppression varies in terms of its intensity and comprehension. Some concepts have shared or common features with other concepts. Concept of suppression is a good example. While suppression, oppression, repression, subjugation, silencing, deprivation, coercion, restriction, enslavement, limitation and others have shared aspects or dimensions, they also differ in terms of other aspects or dimensions. Political, cultural, economic and psychological contexts in a given place and time determine the form of suppression that fits a certain context. While a certain concept may be specifically mentioned in the following treatment, statements and conclusions may be true of the other related concepts in as much as the context or meaning allows.

Taysir Nashif
July 2011   Hamilton, NJ

TNNashif@aol.com

The Global System
and Sub-Systems

A global system or a sub-system is conditioned by the interaction among variable factors and is influenced by the extent of the presence-influence of the political variable. Any act, action, activity, statement, idea, need, want, individual, group, expectation, poverty, aspiration, myth, legend, belief, history, religion, tradition, sect, national sense, ethnicity, perception, misperception, influence, culture, circumstance, pressure, politics, policy, strategy, plan, project, tactic, state, government, legitimacy, illegitimacy, dictation, season, sense of dignity, oppression, wealth, social gap, status, stratification or lack of any of which is a variable factor.

A system is a combination of knowingly or unknowingly interrelated, interdependent and interacting variable factors that exert influence and/ or cause the performance of hidden and/or unknown functions, leading to the formation of a collective entity with a control mechanism that significantly helps the variable factors perform their functions. This control mechanism is politics. "Politics," as defined here, is use of means to acquire the ability of influence needed to achieve certain goals.

Politics is the dominant variable or factor in a system. No other variable, such as professionalism, ethics, knowledge, objectivity or analysis, can match the influence generated by politics; that is because of the fact that politics is in the nature of man, is the dominant factor in human attitude and behavior, is subtle (sneaky) and is less sensitive to non-political factors. A factor in the global system which is supported by political influence is a factor which enjoys the upper hand.

A global system is one where the political factor plays a major role in, or exercises a major influence on, or has a bigger presence in, determining the functionality of the other factors in the system. The characterization of a given system as global, major, big or a sub-system depends on the extent of effect of the political factor vis-a-vis the other factors in determining the proportion of each factor in bringing about the extent of the factors' influence in the system, in determining the relations among the various factors, and in determining the significance of each factor in that system.

The source of the political factor may be wealth, genealogy, finance, thought, nepotism, friendship, legitimacy, learning, occupation, specialization, charisma, enjoyment of exercise of power and authority, policy, plan, strategy, or any combination of these and of other factors.

The influence of these sources and others is a result, to varying degrees, of the political factor. Each factor, or its absence, is political, in the sense that it exercises an influence on the other factors, with its presence or absence. The statement that a present factor exercises an influence is more understandable than a statement that an absent factor exercises an influence. The influence of an absent factor comes about by the fact that its absence influences the nature of the interaction of the present and the other absent factors. In this case, with the absence of a factor, the result of the interaction is different. This statement actually means that the absent factor is present with its "absence" or that the absence is a form of presence

Whereas politics is exercised in all conceivable fields, it is more present, pronounced or dominant in some fields, for example, mayoralty of a town, than in others. Politics is more evident, for instance, in government, management and state affairs than in the process of fishing or skiing. Also, there are fields which more lend themselves to politics than do others. Parliamentary or local elections more lend themselves to politics than taking a cruising trip.

There is a global system, which includes sub-systems. Within a sub-system there are also sub-sub-systems. What determines a system's being global or a sub-system is the political presence or lack of it. The Southwest Asian and North African area, for example, is a sub-system which is part of the global system.

There are varying degrees of interrelatedness and interaction among these factors. Thus, the impact of the factors in each sub-system or of the global system is dynamically varying. A system is not the factors present only; it is, rather, besides the present factors, the absent factors in their influence with their various and varying degree of strength. Occurrence of an influence of a so-called absent factor on present variable factors makes that "absent" factor a present factor.

According to this model of a system, variable factors are relevant and internal. Their relevance makes them internal. There are no irrelevant or external factors. To describe a factor as irrelevant or external disqualifies it as a factor. Some factors are essentially political. Other factors are not essentially political: objectivity, analysis, professionalism, distinction between objective and subjective factors, through explanation, knowledge, expertise, skills, logic, science and technology are not essentially political. Yet, in these characteristics, which contain a greater presence of the objective, is inherent a political presence.

To say that a system is global or that there is a sub-system does not mean that a factor, of less or more political nature, in a sub-system is not likely to influence the global system or other sub-systems. It is by nature of the factor to leave its influence not only within its limits, but also beyond its limits to other sub-systems and the global system. Because of the dynamic interaction among the various absent or present factors, producing system-related inputs and outputs, there is, and there can be, no steady, firm, definite or clear-cut boundary or limit among sub-systems and between the sub-systems and the global system. This feature, namely, that influence of a sub-system transcends its "boundaries" to other sub-systems, is also one of the factors of the global system and the sub-systems.

Because of the various and varying factors, with their various and varying influences, with their absence or presence, predictability of forms of configurations of factors and of their influences is difficult to achieve.

What considerably determines "boundaries" is the extent of politics at play at various and varying degrees in combinations of interactive factors with their influence.

Of the various factors, living ones are more active than non-living ones. Humans and human institutions are more relevant for sub-systems and the global system and their structures and survival, more interconnected, dynamic and political than non-human factors.

Excluded or non-perceived factors do have influence on the global system and the sub-systems. Lack of knowledge of factors makes perception of known factors incomplete, causing imbalance in the look at the causal structure of the system. As a system comprises interactive factors, this influence is significant for the interaction and dynamics of the factors of the systems. Lack of knowledge of all factors perhaps gives the known factors more presence in the dynamic structure of the system.

What makes factors or lack of them of more or less influence on a given system is the result of the interaction among the totality of factors and the absence and lack of knowledge of the existence of other factors. Lack of knowledge of the impact of abject poverty, for instance, may cause a certain group to call less attention to poverty. The impact of these and other factors is not only various, but is also varying. Given the constant total interaction and, hence, dynamism, among the factors, they constantly experience change in strength of relations and inter-relations. The extent of the influence of these factors on the condition of a system is a result of their constant interaction. Given the variability of the influence of these factors, the condition of a system is in a state of flux.

The criteria for the existence of a system are: (1) identity of the subject-matters of the factors at play; (2) the scope of the space or area covered by the subject-matters; (3) and, more importantly, the strength of the presence of the political factor. As mentioned earlier, this political factor is inherent in the nature of the subject-matter, or somehow influencing the subject-matter. This influence takes place as a result of the dynamic interaction of all of the factors at play, with their presence or absence, in a system.

To have a system with many seen and unseen, absent and present, on a short and long span of time, of universal or less universal factors, interacting with each other, means it is a complex system. This complexity has a say in the extent, or the speed of the occurrence, of the resultant influences of such dynamic factors.

The factors—whether more or less political—in a system are consequential, in the sense that the presence of a factor influences the dynamic presence of the other factors. Because of the unevenness of the political influence, the extent of a factor in a system being influenced or influencing does vary. A sub-system may, sometimes, be able to perform its function and to prevent the performance of another sub-system's function. This prevention would be a factor in creating factors in the prevented sub-system where an increased political focus would be likely to lead in the future to more influence on the preventing sub-system.

In such a dynamic system, there is no certainty in performance of functions. Functions differ one from the other in the extent of their likelihood of being performed. In order to make the performance of functions more likely or less likely, there is a need to have increase or decrease—whatever the case may be—in the influence of factors that work in the desired direction. Given the varying degrees of influence of factors—as a result of their dynamic interaction—some factors—due to their substance, content or relevance—may have a greater or lesser influence in making the performance of the function more or less likely. This likelihood or lack of it may range from whatever low percent to whatever high percent.

Because of the precisely unpredictable configuration of the interdependent factors in a system, some statements concerning them are not made in absolute, certain, or categorical terms, but in relative, probabilistic terms. Still, this element of relativity and probability can reach that high degree of probability that there is an almost certainty of action or lack of it.

Factors in the system differ in terms of their political quality. Some factors are essentially political. Their dominant intended function is political. They purposely have to do with the performance of a political role, of seeking, through various means, to acquire influence in order to achieve certain goals.

There are factors with each of them integrates both the political and the non-political aspects or components. Medicine, engineering and mathematics, for example, are essentially non-political; yet, there is a political aspect in their application. Exact sciences, professionalism, analysis, explanation, theorization, objectivity, for instance, are factors where there is a greater degree of non-political component and a lesser degree of political component. Within the factor, the two aspects or components are in a dynamic state of conflict or competition. With reading out poems, for instance, a poet is performing a function of being a poet and a political function of spreading contents, ideas, ideals, admiration and fame, which are political. When a presence of the essentially political component and of less-political component exercise their influence in a system, a dynamic relation between the essentially political and the less political aspects is created where both engage in the assertion of existence vis-à-vis the other. This is especially so when both or more than two are performing a common function. An example of this case is the medical and political function of attempting to promote public health.

The political dimension of a factor—which has an influence on the dynamic interaction of factors in a system—does sometimes have a decisive influence on that interaction. Some factors with their political dimensions, then, have a far-reaching say in the direction or orientation of the system: in policy, political, or strategic formulation.

Factors can, at the same time, be both dependent and independent: for example, attitude can be dependent on a socio-cultural environment, and independent, in the sense of influencing political behavior. The dependence and independence themselves are resultant of the overall dynamically interactive factors in the system. Because of this interaction, the extent of a factor being dependent or independent does vary. Whatever the factors in the systems may be, the political dimension is always there.

To be judgmental about the realities of the systemic factors means a disregard or lack of sensitivity of the influence resulting from the reality of the dynamic interaction of such a system.

Given the multitude of interactive more political and less political factors, there can never be equilibrium in the global system or sub-systems. Inequalities are always bound to emerge from this interaction. A goal needs to be available to try to reduce inequality. To achieve this goal, influence needs to be exercised by more influential factors—such as people of authority—to position the system in such a manner as to reduce the inequality. Otherwise, tension and friction are bound to linger.

In order to make a result of the interaction more likely to be predictable or less likely to be unpredictable, the less political factors, such as professionalism, analysis and objectivity, need to have more presence in the system of the interactive factors, and the more political factor should have less presence in that system. This statement is also true of the interactive factors in the sub-systems.

Politics and Influence

The human being is a political creature. Politics is inherent in the nature of man, his behavior and life. Politics is action to acquire ability to exercise influence in order to achieve goals. Politics in this sense is wider than the concept of politics as leadership of states and management of government. Each activity is political, because in it is inherent the exercise of influence.

Relations between human beings in various fields are political, in the sense that they involve exercise of influence and are being influenced. Educational, economic, international relations are political. In every relation between two peoples or between two states there is a political factor.

The strength of the political dimension in the human activity varies depending on the various cultural, psychological, historical and natural circumstances of the human being. One of such circumstances is professional specialization. The stronger is one's professional specialization, the weaker is the political dimension in his professional performance. But, at the same time, his political weight as a person who is performing a function in society increases. His professional functionality in society secures his exercise of influence. The size of this influence depends on factors, such as the extent of respect enjoyed by a certain profession in society.

The considerations of the assumption of power and of sustaining such assumption are existent in all of the political systems in the whole world. Such systems differ one from the other in terms of the importance attached to such considerations. Given this situation, accommodation of the results of research is limited by these two considerations. Hence, governmental and non-governmental authorities' adoption of such results is expected to be incomplete. Governmental bodies, by virtue of their acquisition of the means of influence and coercion, are able in democratic, quasi-democratic and despotic systems, especially in non-democratic systems, to intervene in the various domains of the human life, to direct societies' activities towards the direction that they want, to devise order of priorities in the management of the affairs of society, people and state and to violate the laws. In doing that governmental bodies are prompted by motives, the more important of which is retaining of its interests, including the interest of assumption of power and its maintenance.

In policy formulation, the extent of benefit from results of social research (in the comprehensive sense, namely the political, cultural, economic and psychological aspects) has relation to the nature of the political system. The more important the assumption of power is in the formulation and implementation of policy, the more marginalized is the result of such research.

A factor in the performance of professions can be dealt with from a different perspective. In such performance the importance of the political factor increases or decreases depending on whether the professional specialization is in the mathematical, logical and natural sciences—the exact sciences—or in the less exact sciences, such as law, sociology and political science.

It is of the nature of the less exact sciences that they more lend themselves to interpretation and in their propositions there is a greater share of subjectivity and judgment. By contrast are the more exact sciences which are less subject to interpretations. In the professional performance, which is based on specialization in the exact sciences, there is a lesser amount of political presence because here is a lesser presence, in this performance, of the personal subjective interpretation, thus allowing to the specialist more room for the exercise of influence.

A long legacy of subjugation to foreign rule, of political autocracy, and of social oppression has buttressed and continues to buttress political tyranny. Social oppression is expressed or manifested in such institutions as patriarchal system, political monopoly and nepotism.

Convergence of interests, such as continued exercise of authority and buttressing the authority structure, is one factor for the emergence of alliances between persons with political authority and those who assume authority in these and other institutions. Relations between members of both groups sometimes go beyond of the character of alliance into merger of those who constitute the socio-political structure that occupies the very top of the socio-political hierarchy.

Political reality in Western countries has shown that democratic institutions are not able to properly function under the pressure of economic pressures, non-democratic ideology and lobbyists with no commitment to democratic values.

Democracy and political freedom lend themselves to be maneuvered in such as a way as to be utilized by a few to promote their anti-freedom and undemocratic goals. Abuse of democracy and freedom has been and still is facilitated by a number of factors such as poverty, reading and functional illiteracy, a strong and long legacy of people's subjugation to political tyranny, social oppression and foreign rule, lack of familiarity of people with the practice of democracy, presence of strong ideological forces with anti-democratic agendas.

This statement supports the argument that in order to achieve a desired change and development, a comprehensive approach should be adopted, in the sense that all factors that are relevant for a certain goal should be accommodated simultaneously.

Culture and Western Cultural Influence

Culture has various definitions. Of these two more important definitions are as follows: culture is mainly the manner of communication people follow and the manner of their dealing one with the others and with things and phenomena. The other definition is that culture is mainly the ideals and values which are adopted by people. The two definitions have some identical and similar features. A popular culture is drawn from the ideological, intellectual, historical, psychological and geographical space of the people.

Concepts, which deal with a certain semantic field, have certain similarities and differences. While having an emphasis on certain aspects of a semantic field, contents in that field share certain semantic similarities. Oppression, limitation, fanaticism, intellectual dichotomy, bigotry and others in their respective semantic fields share certain similarities and divergences. Hence, a statement guided by a certain concept within one semantic field applies, to various and varying degrees, to other concepts.

In the shadow of the miserable conditions that considerably hinder achievement of progress in the developing world, cultural change needs to be made. It is impossible to convert the potential of the developing peoples into a reality without eliminating the factors that hinder progress.

Some of the reasons for underdevelopment are as follows: the insignificant role played by science in the life of societies; the role played by institutions benefiting from the existing circumstances in deemphasizing of the importance of science and technology or in giving inadequate incentive to it; a considerable degree of intellectual inertia and incomprehensibility; governmental and non-governmental authority; the masculine patriarchal system; the system of inculcating education which lays emphasis on memorization, and the negligence of independent and creative thought; hostility to philosophical thought or paying less deserved consideration;

the major role played by the clannish, tribal and sectarian organization; feudalism; the system of *shilla* (members of a group interconnected by certain interests) in the various countries; lack of courage among many Muslims to point at the Muslim misunderstanding of the text of the Qur'an and Prophet Muhammad's Sayings and Doings (*as-Sunna*), and the lack of adequate understanding of concepts, such as predetermination, penalty, man's accountability for his actions, God's vicar ship of man on the Earth, indifference, enchantment with the Western person, negative influence exercised by the static thought, insignificant role played by active and critical thought, Western cultural invasion which has disrupted the smooth, natural development process, to a certain extent, of thought.

Westernization and cultural identity of the developing countries have been the subject of discussion in the professional literature. In this literature Westernization has been taken as a driving force for cultural change. Some analysts in the developing world have portrayed Westernization as follows: To consider the West as the eternal teacher and the non-West as the eternal student, as only model for each civilization progress, and as representing the whole of humanity and Europe as the center of weight in it.

What is happening is the creation of isolated cultural centers among the non-Western peoples, with these centers supporting the West or serving as bodies that are in the process of becoming supportive of it. Such centers, when coming to assume authority, act to turn educational Westernization into a political process, causing split and confrontation between the peoples. Innovation used by non-Western peoples are attributed to the West. Western mentality is one that is creating patterns of general and universal thought. Many non-Western cultures have and are becoming civilization agencies and an extension of Western doctrines. Besides, there is a feeling of inferiority complex vis-à-vis the languages, cultures, science, doctrines, views and theories of the West.

These Western influences, which were in the military, economic and imperial fields, were and continue to be a significant factor in bringing about economic and political crisis in the developing countries, slowing down or hampering the process of the normal natural cultural and political development of these countries.

Uniform Lines of Thinking and Intellectual Inconsistency

Uniform lines of thinking have restrictions on intellectual freedom. Intellectual uniformity is a kind of intellectual suppression, as it only covers the intellectual space affected by that uniformity, and it excludes the intellectual space not accompanied by it. As this uniformity only accepts itself, it does not, nor can it, admit of other intellectual propositions. Uniform line of thinking is one intellectual system. As such, it does not accept other uniform lines of thinking. A uniform line of thinking, which is limited to one intellectual system, excludes other intellectual systems.

Uniform lines of thinking are not necessarily comprehensive or all-embracing. Such lines of thinking are reflections or embodiments of the lack of comprehensive or all-embracing intellectual consistency. In the case of the lack of comprehensive intellectual consistency, as is the case in many uniform lines of thinking, the uniform line of thinking would be inconsistent with other such uniform lines. The lack of consistency of a certain uniform line of thinking with other uniform lines of thinking is one of the main reasons for intellectual compartmentalization, fragmentation and polarization at the intellectual, cultural and social levels. Passing judgment on things, disregarding the fact of the ignorance of such things, is suppression of the existence of such things.

Thought has witnessed and is still witnessing many uniform lines of thinking. These have taken various forms, including inflexible political and economic doctrines and ideologies, such as sectarianism, fascism, Nazism, racism, communism, survival of the fittest and white man's carrying of the message or burden of the spread of democracy and civilization in the world. They have also taken the following forms: deterministic tendency, restrictive linguist formulas, lack of accommodation of the dynamism of social phenomena, intellectual impenetrability, feeling of intellectual sufficiency, and intellectual absolutism are uniform lines of thinking.

Uniform lines of thinking took on the forms of political and economic ideologies and doctrines. Examples of such uniform lines abound: the view that people's happiness is necessarily enhanced with technological development; wealth is the biggest source of assurance; multitude of children is a guarantee of happiness; the view that thought is objective and that social sciences are neutral; the view that the Aryan mind is superior and more developed than the non-Aryan one; the view that women lack the ability to manage the world. It is probably clear that such way of thinking does not take into account the reality and is restrictive and exclusivist, hence it involves intellectual suppression of the aspects of which that uniform line of thinking does not take account. To confine human happiness to technological development, notwithstanding the appreciation of the importance of this factor, involves intellectual restriction and exclusion, as such limitation excludes the conception of the realization of happiness without technological development. Also, there are sources of assurance other than material wealth. Children may be a source of concern instead of being a source of happiness.

Strict pursuit of uniform line of thinking means lack of intellectual flexibility; it means lack of sensitivity towards contents emanating from semantic proposition of that uniform line of thinking. Uniform line of thinking does not take into account the smaller contents that the uniform line of thinking does not cover.

In order for thought to be out of the frame of uniform line of thinking, this line needs to be broken through analysis and deconstruction of the reality which is complex by its nature. A thing cannot be understood without its analysis. Through it, it becomes clear the impenetrability and the restriction of the uniform line of thought, and it also becomes clear that uniform line of thinking prevents penetration into the fold of reality with its many active and interactive dimensions. With breaking the uniform line of thinking, thought is enhanced. Domination of the uniform line of thinking, which is dominant, to various extents, over all peoples and individuals, is one basic reason for the intellectual and mental stalemate from which they suffered. Analysis, because of its not taking consideration of the dynamism of a phenomenon, is only sufficient, to a certain extent, to break that line.

To analysis and deconstruction critical approach is linked. With these three factors, there would be disenchantment with myths, falsehoods, feeble-mindedness, intellectual hypocrisy, flattery and vanities that are currently widespread in different layers of human society. These and others are a thick barrier that hides truth from being seen. Such a barrier would be eliminated only through deconstruction and adoption of the critical approach, as with both of these factors, thought and behavior become more rational, systematic and logical. With them, it would become easier to know intellectual and cultural sources that are more beneficial to people, and for the human being to better understand reality.

These uniform lines of thinking are manifestations of generalized intellectual inconsistency. This inconsistency is a main factor for intellectual "pocketing," fragmentation, polarization and division on the intellectual, social and cultural levels. The uniform line of thinking is not necessarily comprehensive. When it is not comprehensive, the uniform line of thinking may be inconsistent with other uniform lines of thinking, which may also be incomprehensive. The uniform line of thinking that "thought is objective" cannot be consistent with the uniform line of thinking that "developing peoples are culturally underdeveloped." And the uniform line of thinking that "social sciences are neutral" is inconsistent with the uniform line of thinking that "mind is the only tool with which to know creation."

In order for thought to get rid of the frame of intellectual uniformity, this uniform structure should be broken down through understanding, analysis and deconstruction of the complex reality. Understanding contains analysis; it cannot be achieved without analysis. Breaking down intellectual uniformity would lead to intellectual liberation. Through this analysis, the impenetrability, narrowness and limitation of uniformity become clear.

In view of the fact that it is not possible to understand the nature of relations between individuals, groups and states without explanation that takes into account both the mental and spiritual dimensions of such relations, then uniform lines of thinking have delayed and continue to delay progress of the social sciences and to limit human knowledge.

Prohibitions—or taboos—are a uniform line of thought. In prohibiting what is the subject of prohibition, they restrict and suppress that which is forbidden. A multitude of prohibitions in society indicates a strong social and intellectual tendency towards intellectual and emotional impenetrability and restriction. In more interactive and open-minded societies there are fewer prohibitions, as through intellectual interaction and open-mindedness people will understand the mythical basis and futility of some prohibitions and will have a better appreciation of the value of nature and freedom.

A society with fewer prohibitions is closer to a natural state and to the exercise of a greater freedom and closer to intellectual openness. It is a society in which human individualism is more likely to be stronger and more genuine. That is because the essence of nature rejects restriction, because prohibition negates freedom and restricts thought, which by nature tends to be free, and because prohibition is a clear intervention in man's administering of his own life, and thus an infringement of one's individualism.

By his nature, man has a strong inclination to freedom and to achieve himself and his individuality. He, thus, cannot be restricted by a number of legal and social restrictions. Hence, he might not be sensitive secretly or publicly to such restrictions, what could bring about confusion. This situation might lead some people to partiality and false conformity. This situation might indicate imbalance in the followed system of prohibition. In order to extricate individuals from this psychological and behavioral dilemma it is necessary to remove the prohibitions which are unneeded socially, culturally and value-wise, and it is necessary to get the legal systems back to perform their original functions, namely, to facilitate for people to administer the affairs of their lives.

Intellectual Dichotomy

In a considerable part of thought, all people have what may be called intellectual dichotomy. Its nature, which is found in various manifestations in all parts of the world, is that it is impenetrable, hence rigid and characterized with inertia. Intellectual dichotomy forms a restriction on thought, because such dichotomy does not take into account, nor does it match, intellectual dynamism, the dynamics of the complex reality of life and the changing human understanding with the change of life circumstances. The interaction of the multiple factors of reality necessarily tends to go beyond the limits of intellectual dichotomy. Impenetrability, emanating from intellectual dichotomy, is limited to thought without that thought having room for the intellectual dynamism of reality and without having that thought going beyond the scope of the dichotomous thought. With its dichotomy, thought is impenetrable. Being impenetrable, it is frozen, hence it does not, nor can it accommodate intellectually the potential and probabilities of the dynamic thought. Intellectual activity is wider than intellectual dichotomy. Complexity of reality means multitude of factors of the reality whose interaction necessarily leads them to go beyond intellectual dichotomy.

To conceive the model of Western development, for example, and of development of any people as contradictory is one which gives evidence to ignorance of such models, as in the various models there must be, because of the unity of human nature, some similar and identical aspects.

According to this thought, the existence of something is conceived as negating the existence of its opposite. Hence, conflicts arise between opposite intellectual currents. Conflicts arise when an individual or a group which supports a certain current is prevented from expressing its ideas by a group which supports an opposite current.

Intellectual dichotomy is reflected in the exclusivist thought, which, in turn, is reflected in the phenomenon of the full refusal or absolute acceptance of a concept. From intellectual dichotomy emanate ideas of excluding the disagreeing, and, what is worse, the different, in various fields in all societies. This exclusion varies in terms of extremity or weakness according to the nature of the culture of peoples. Examples abound on this mentality: writers exclude or make attempts to exclude other writers who have different and disagreeing positions and views; supporters of change keep distance from those who call for keeping heritage. Such splits take place, in spite of the facts that, in many cases, there are points of agreement between the seemingly fully opposite phenomena.

This pattern of thought places a burden on the efforts of those who are trying to achieve a gradual change while keeping social coherence. Because of the dynamic intellectual and cultural interaction, there is no full contradiction between what seems to be intellectually contradictory phenomena. Secularism, modernization, Islamic thought, socialism, capitalism, nationalism, liberalism, social solidarity, and others are not completely mutually exclusive. All these currents share similar objective and subjective aspects. Additionally, in the ancient Egyptian, Sumerian, Assyrian, Indian, Chinese, Persian, Greek, Roman, Arabic-Islamic, and contemporary thought there are similar and shared aspects. All over the world, concepts, such as government, fairness, law, justice, limits, controls, freedom, goals, means, specialization, competence, professionalism, society, human being, individual, gender, state, science, banner, research, need, insights, experience, economy, happiness, misery, expectation and others, have universal shared semantic meaning.

In fact, the mental conception can cover the full gamut of a thing, from one edge to its extreme other edge. Any color has various shades. There are always various colors between the black and the white, and various points between the low and the high physically and morally; there are, likewise, various extents or degrees between the rich and the poor, between bigotry and tolerance, knowledge and ignorance, enmity and friendship, hatred and love.

Intellectual bigotry involves intellectual restriction, as bigotry involves exclusion of what is not covered by that bigotry. As scientific and philosophical thought does not accept intellectual restriction, intellectual bigotry contradicts thought.

On the global social and cultural arena, conflicts are emerging and going on between currents, sects, trends and groupings around secularism, modernization, heritage, Western thought, traditional thought and others and about their approval or disapproval of their adoption or adoption a portion of their aspects. One major reason for this conflict is lack of the unity of word in the social sense which includes contents of culture, politics, society, economy and also, more specifically, because of lack of framework within which an individual or a group supporting this or that current can express its opinions and struggle to spread them without fear for their lives from the wrath and vengeance of followers of other currents.

This conflict also indicates a considerable amount of ignorance. Objectively, it is impossible for such currents to fully exclude each other. Such currents have intellectual, objective and ideological aspects that are interwoven with each other. Capitalism, socialism, liberalism, interdependence, social solidarity, heritage, modernization, issues of love, concepts of life, law society, human relations, marriage, family, happiness, enjoyment have some common aspects, and each of them have aspects that do not exclude some aspects in other currents. Such aspects from various social and cultural currents can interact with each other, and it is unavoidable that some aspects of them are similar or identical. In the ancient Egyptian, Sumerian, Assyrian, Chinese, Hindu, Greek, Roman, Islamic and Arabic thought and in the contemporary thought in the various parts of the globe there are the concepts of governance, law, equity, prohibitions, controls, freedom, target, goal, means, specialization, society, the human being, individual, race, state, science, banner, research, need, insight, economization, prosperity and misery which have some common aspects.

To conceive the Western model of development, for example, and the Islamic model of development, or the developmental model of any people, as contradictory, evinces inadequacy of the understanding of the reality of development. Because of the unity of human nature, in any model of development there should be similar or identical aspects of such models.

As a matter of fact, intellectual conceptions can cover the full range or continuum of a certain thing, from the beginning of one side to the extreme end of the other side. Each color has many shades. Also, there are many shades between two colors, such as black and white. For a site located between the low and the high there are many points. This is true also with respect to poverty, wealth, richness, intolerance, knowledge, ignorance, enmity, friendliness, hatred, love, and also between backing of, and opposition to, modernization with its Western model and with its Islamic model.

To say that the characteristic of the human history is only the conflict of civilizations involves intellectual suppression. With viewing the conflict of civilizations as the only factor in the human history, other factors in history are arbitrarily excluded.

Related to dichotomy is exaggeration, which contains extremism and extreme bias, involves intellectual suppression. Exaggeration in treatment of something in a certain way prevents taking into account dimensions of that thing that are not covered by the concern of one who is led by his exaggeration to neglect those dimensions. Exaggeration in the adoption or application of any social system, such as capitalism, communism, nationalism, or any tendency, such as individualism, consumerism, materialism, or a sense of superiority, comes at the expense of other phenomena which are necessarily excluded by the extremism of the exaggerating person in that adoption or application. Given that an individual neglects, when adopting or applying an aspect of a concept, other aspects, exaggeration is not the ideal method in achieving understanding between the human beings. Aspects of a phenomenon have active and mutual relations. By limiting attention to some aspects of the phenomenon, without attention to the other aspects, would be a deficient understanding of the phenomenon. Given the fact that value-directed bias is one of the reasons for such a limitation, then that limitation is permeated by subjective and value-ridden motives.

Because of the extreme, suppressive and exclusivist character of exaggeration, it causes social and psychological congestion which leads to deprivation, tensions, disputes and destruction. Excesses of the capitalist tendency in the West have increased the materialistic and individualistic tendencies and consumerism, have led to excesses in those tendencies, and have weakened the spiritual dimension. This situation in its totality has strengthened the negative implications on the health of the human social fabric at both the local and world levels.

Intellectual Conservatism
and Dynamics of Reality

Intellectual conservatism is a uniform line of thinking. Conservative thought is less compatible with creativity and open-mindedness. Such conservatism lacks the tendency to intellectual change, discovery, creativity and imagination. By its nature, intellectual conservatism seeks to be conservative with respect to existing thought, while inherent in creativity and open-mindedness are renewal of thought, expansion of its scope and change of the existing thought that may have become irrelevant to people's values and needs.

Impenetrability of a uniform line of thinking means that it is restricted to a certain thought without that thought being capable of having room for the intellectual dynamism of reality. This uniformity is limited by its inability to allow thought to travel beyond the scope of the uniform. Being impenetrable, it is inflexible, and, consequently, it does not make room intellectually for the possibilities of active thinking. This uniformity, because it does not take account of—nor does it keep up with—the dynamism of thought, the complex reality of life and the human understanding which is changing with the change of circumstances of life, is restrictive and suppressive.

Intellectual activity is wider than a line of thinking. Complexity of reality intellectually goes beyond uniform intellectual scope. Complexity of reality means the multitude of factors of reality whose interaction necessarily goes beyond one line of thinking. Understanding complex reality necessitates departure from one line of thinking and a rebellion against the restrictive approach of adopting one line of thinking.

A factor that contributes to increase in awareness is pursuit of deconstruction. Social context is an intellectual, ideological and mythological one. People think with a group of values, principles, beliefs and assumptions, and a group of legends, superstitions and delusions.

Ideology and mythology (which includes legends and superstitions) interact with each other and influence people's thought and life.

Given the fact that ideological thought is narrower than reality, then generalization of any ideological-mythological thought would certainly be at the expense of the understanding of reality. Given the tendency on the part of the ideological, theoretical and mythological structures of the human thinking to abstraction, generalization, extremism, partiality and excess of self-confidence, then such structures hide the human reality partially or completely. Generalization of such structures is, then, suppression of reality. In order to remove such suppression, it is necessary to pursue the deconstructionist method which, by its nature, removes delusion, ambiguity and magic from thought and from reality.

Of the most important objectives of legal systems and social institutions are enabling people to undertake, being inspired by their values and beliefs, to manage the affairs of their lives and to facilitate this management. Those who are in charge of the affairs in the state or society in the whole world have a tendency to go beyond the objectives of the existence of such systems and institutions. In all societies, those in charge actually go beyond the two above-mentioned objectives to intervene in the intellectual activity, to try, often successfully, to change the human value system, and prohibit many of the human activities in domains that do not fall within the range of these institutions. Performance of all human institutions has negative and positive results, with varying rates of the difference in these results. Not a few of such institutions are corrupt, corrupting and/or have deteriorating character of corruption. To think otherwise is a kind of illusion, naiveté or ignorance. Even when there are positive results in a major part of an institution's performance of functions, in time the portion of the negative aspects increase.

Many human institutions, to say the least, limit human ability to develop the natural tendency to do good deeds, realization of happiness with no excessive limitations and curb man's ability to develop his mind and thought. Institutions, in their majority, restrict intellectual freedom, human activity, human tendency to intellectual and psychological emancipation and creative elevation to higher spiritual levels.

Many social institutions cause growth of bias, partiality, prejudice, bigotry, narrow mindedness and attention to trivialities. They promote narrow mindedness and impede independence, progress and sense of personal privacy.

There are reasons for the particularly corrupt governmental institutions. The more important of such reasons is that such institutions possess a great deal of ability, being institutions of implementation and coercion, for forceful enforcement and to impose their will. Government and its bodies are major obstacles that obstruct the road to man's realization of himself. They are a more important factor in raping the individual conscience and in distancing the human being from his natural state of self, in encroaching on himself and on his psychological cohesion.

One of the most important ways in which human institutions differ one from the other is the strength of the political nature of the institution's functions, and the strength of the political nature of its relations with other institutions. Political nature of relations between institutions means that in these relations the political factor has influence.

The political nature of functions means that performance of the function involves use of various legal, psychological and economic ways and use of means which draw their strength from the values, traditions, customs and heritage in order to achieve performance of the function.

Of the many human institutions, governmental institutions, their functions and their relations to other institutions and to people are of a stronger political nature, because of the nature of the governmental institutions, one of whose functions is exercise of governing in society. Hence, such relations involve a greater deal of pressure and coercion, as performance of the governing function requires, from the viewpoint of rulers, obedience of the governed and their compliance with the rulers' directives and orders.

Dichotomy and Science, Philosophy and Logic

Non-scientific thought can be ideological or mythological. To put ideological or mythological thought above other kinds of thought comes inescapably at the expense of the understanding of reality, because this thought is narrower than reality. This thought hides—slightly or significantly—human reality. When truth is faced against a background of reality, the irrelevance of those structures for the understanding of reality becomes clear.

What would contribute to the elimination or weakening of intellectual dichotomy is to make thought more scientific, rational, philosophical and logical. Through penetration of philosophical, logical, scientific and rational thought in the lives of peoples it would be possible to change the way people think. Such a thought would create and increase awareness of the multiplicity of the dimensions of phenomenon, of the multitude of alternatives and options, of the relativity of concepts, of the extent of the strength or weakness of a phenomenon, of the limitedness of human knowledge, and of the validity of the statement that difference in opinion should not mean encroachment on the human dignity.

Philosophical thought, which can be hypothetical or unverified, and scientific thought, which is verifiable and explanatory, can provide options and alternatives. Availability of a larger number of options and alternatives would further contribute to weaken extreme and dichotomous thought. Promotion of philosophical thought would be promotion of intellectual freedom and it would provide the opportunity to enter worlds that were not entered by scientific thought.

Some peoples and cultures have a bias against philosophical thinking. The reason for this bias is ignorance, socialization which goes hand in hand with familiar and usual things and belief of certain intellectual currents that teaching of philosophy might encroach on the strength of some traditional intellectual orientations.

Intellectual dichotomy, which restricts intellectual freedom, contradicts with scientific thought which does not accept intellectual restriction.

General intellectual reference system is monopolistic, in the sense that it does not allow other reference systems to operate within the existing general reference system. General intellectual reference system may have a geographical level and/or a thematic level. With this intellectual monopoly, it is the central and hegemonic reference system. To serve as a general intellectual and predominant reference system means that other intellectual output is dominated by it and subject to it. Acceptance of centrality of an intellectual referential system means a dichotomous division of people into those who serve as upholders of referential thought, and those whose intellectual output is subordinate to the referential thought. Those of the subordinated intellectual output are regarded intellectually inconsequential by virtue of the dictation of the intellectual monopolistic referential system, a state in which is inherent social coercion and injustice.

Each individual has his varying share of knowledge in various fields and his intellectual faculty of judgment, and of his ethical commitment. The monopolization of the authority of interpreting sources of reference impairs the legitimate bases for the claim of right to have people's intellectual-ethical makeup given their due weight and place in the interpretation of sources of reference.

This monopolistic approach is ethically defective, as, ethically speaking, no one has the absolute authority to claim monopolistic right to such interpretation coming at the expense of others who are ethically entitled to claim right of authority to such an interpretation.

As there is a subjective component in every human understanding, including interpretation, it would be presumptuous to attribute full objectivity, completeness and truth to any human understanding. An indication of that is the fact that individual understanding is different or contradictory. As understanding consists of ideology, interests, and considerations which are not subjective-free, no two understandings are identical.

This mental dichotomy, the mental division into two extremes is not realistic; it is an abstract, ideal, mental entity. Mental entities, which seem contradictory in the mental domain, have a wide space for convergence and a long range of degrees in between the two extremes.

Relativity and Multiplicity
of Dimensions

A feature of correct thought is that it is a relative, not absolute, thought, that acknowledges intellectual multilateralism and multitude of intellectual alternatives related to a particular question. One feature of a developed society is that, in the behavior of its individuals or of a large section of them, recognition of intellectual multilateralism and of the existence of intellectual alternatives and options exercises effect on the behavior of the members of society.

Multilateralism is an important tool for the achievement of goals, such as social balance and the availability of opportunities at the social plane and equality between genders. Extremism contradicts with multilateralism, because the starting point of multilateralism is inclusion, social affiliation and openness to accept others and their thought, whereas bigotry is limited to an intellectual or human portion of the human and intellectual totality and it is far ways from human and intellectual inclusion and refuses openness.

On the level of empirical reality, there is no such thing as a full adjective. As full adjective is ideal, it does not exist and is unachievable. Such adjectives or nouns, as a specialist, scientist, objective, are relative. An adjective is relative to other persons. The adjective of a person is also relative, depending on our perceptions, misperceptions, judgments, interpretations, understanding and biases. That adjective is also relative to the abstract, ideal adjective which, by its being abstract and ideal, is not in existence and unachievable. By the same token, as there is no full adjective, there is no complete stupidity, or full ignorance. There is no person who does not make mistakes.

In the world of sensual perceptions there is nothing with absolute quality. Absolute thought is not consistent with relative thought. For thought to be pluralistic, it must be relative. Absolute thought is intellectual bigotry. Attribution of a full adjective to the described thing is intellectual extremism and dichotomy. For instance, to attribute full beauty to something is absolute thought because it described that thing as having full beauty. This is a bigoted idea, because by attributing full beauty to something, the quality of ugliness in it was disregarded. This also applies to attribution of full democracy to the so-called democratic regime, and the attribution of full freedom to press. From the departing point of the relativity of the adjectives of things, there is no democratic regime one hundred per cent, nor is there freedom of the press one hundred per cent in any place in the world. And there is no full objectivity or neutrality in study. Examples of bigotry is to consider something as full insane or sane, as full evil or full goodness, and as full virtue or vile. Between two absolute contrasts, for example, courage and cowardice, progress and backwardness, love and hatred, there are countless degrees falling in between both extremes. To attribute a full quality to something means lack of knowledge or lack of adequate knowledge of that thing and, hence, negligence or ignoring what is not known.

Along this line of reasoning, it is wrong to describe the experience of Arab progress as a full failure; it is clear that it is not a full success. It is wrong to say that all Western values or Arab values as good or as bad, or that all aspects of the Arab or Western heritage are good or are bad. It is also wrong to say that there is a full contrast between the Arabic culture and another factor. Also, from the same opinion of the error of adoption of intellectual extremism, it is wrong to say that intellectual currents, such as liberalism, nationalism, secularism capitalism, fully excludes each other or fully accepts each other. Some of the propositions of such currents are similar and others are not similar. Such currents agree, for example, on the concepts of emancipation and of need for preservation of survival.

Lack of acceptance of the idea of the relativity of the qualities of things and the acceptance of the idea of intellectual bigotry and extremism mean narrowing of the margin of intellectual freedom, as intellectual extremism does not allow thought to go beyond one of the two contrasting extremes.

Each idea has its multiple dimensions, aspects or components. Of these dimensions are the historical dimension, the dimension of the circumstances that surround the idea, the dimension of the extent of its understanding, the dimension of its content, and the dimension of the position taken towards it. Of these dimensions, one dimension connects to the others; among them there is interaction. Splitting of dimensions is not allowed, because the influence of one of them depends in terms of weakness or strength on the influences of the other dimensions whose influences change continuously as a result of the interaction among them and also between them and the idea concerned. Through the splitting of dimensions or isolating them one from the other, this quality is ignored, namely, the quality of interaction among dimensions, consequently, the dimensions of an idea are not viewed as constantly interactive, but are viewed as static. This last view deprives us from the understanding of human thought and reality, and that is because the dimensions of an idea are actively interactive by nature.

This will inescapably show that presence of a dimension in an idea is in proportion to the strength or weakness of the presence of its other dimensions. A dimension is dependent and independent at the same time: it is dependent in the sense that the size of its presence depends on the other dimensions, and it is independent in the sense that the presence of the other dimensions depends on the size of its presence. This means that a given dimension is an influencer and influence at the same time. Because of the interaction among these dimensions, and also because of the interaction between the dimensions and the idea, then the size of the presence of each dimension or the extent of the influence exerted by each dimension is in constant change.

Approach of intellectual relativity unavoidably leads to believe in intellectual dynamism, because intellectual relativity means intellectual dynamism, given the fact that intellectual relativity accommodates continuous intellectual change resulting from continuous interaction between the changing human being and the continuous natural, social, economic, cultural and psychological circumstances. What also contradicts with intellectual relativity is thought resulting from, or affected by, bias, partiality, impenetrability, pocketing and "canning."

A characteristic of a considerable amount of the contemporary human speech is certainty; a confident and categorical language; rushing or hastening with passing of judgment; leaving no room or margin for the probability of error in theoretical and philosophical formulations—all these characteristics have weakened or impeded and are still weakening or impeding theoretical and philosophical formulation of thought.

Human speeches vary one from the other in terms of the weakness or strength of its being characterized with these qualities. This variance depends on factors, such as the scientific, cultural and philosophical legacy, and the nature of the system of government: Is it characterized with a greater degree of democracy or of despotism, the nature of interpretation and application of religious texts, and nature of the social system: Is it characterized with a greater degree of class differentiation or dominated by the patriarchal system, or the extent to which man dominates woman and the extent of her dependence on him in various fields of life?

In each society there are people who certainly believe that their ideas are correct. Certainty is absolute. It is a linear thought. With this certainty, no room for questioning and doubt in that certainty is left. Doubt or its probability is contradictory with the absolute. Given that ideas are relative, then certainty contradicts relativity. Given that certainty is absolute and linear, then it does admit of relativity and pluralism. Certainty of ideas results in giving to the certain person intellectual and psychological tranquility and quiet, while belief in relativity of thought would encourage exercise of thinking.

Critical and scientific approach would be enhanced by having as a starting point relativity of ideas, relativity of their correctness, deficiency of human knowledge, the uncertainty of human thought, and the drawback of the adherence to conceived certainties. Belief that people know everything or that there is none that they do not know has hampered scientific and objective treatment of issues. Such belief has slowed down development of knowledge because such adherence forces people to accept or refuse things people might not accept or refuse if they have availed to their mind an attempt to pursue a road to free intellectual activity. To start out from considering a conceived thing as certain without deserving its being considered as certain is tantamount to imposing our consideration predicated on lack of sufficient knowledge of things.

Sanctification of word is associated with belief of the absolutism of ideas. Person who does not believe that he has answers to all the questions is a person whose behavior is associated with belief in the relativity of ideas. He is a person who is not under the illusion of possessing full knowledge.

What is associated with belief in absolutism of ideas is one's belief in the ability to talk about everything, his confidence that his talk is correct, and the fact that he leaves no room or margin for the probability of error of his thought. What is also associated with belief in absolutism of ideas is exercise of thought which evinces lack of realization by one who is thinking of the complexity of the social, psychological and cultural phenomena, and of their dimensions, and his lack of realization of the need for their deconstruction.

In fact, lack of accommodation of the concept of relativity, which is often not taken into consideration in thought and deed, leads to deficiency in the understanding of human thought and reality.

Historicity is sensitivity to the new circumstances with their needs. As such, it is intellectual openness. As historical phenomena are explainable, they are analyzable, understandable and predictable. Thought, being a result of particular circumstances of time, is historical. Proceeding from the historicity of thought, new circumstances require different interpretation, which contains new answers and solutions. As present circumstances differ from those in the past, so interpretations in the present time are different from those in the past.

As it does not take account of new developments and their needs, non-historicity is insensitive to new circumstances. As such, it is a uniform line of thought and, hence, static. Being static, committed to a certain state, condition or beginning, and insensitive to changing circumstances and their needs, it is suppressive.

History needs to be rewritten so that misinformation, misrepresentation, distortion and suppression may be eliminated. There is no perfect civilization. What is needed not only study by the West of non-Western civilizations, but also study by the non-Western world of the Western civilization. Attempts need to be made to show the falsehood of biased judgments on civilizations. Civilization of others should be studied in a more neutral, objective and fair manner. This would help peoples to make their contributions to world civilization.

Ideality and Dynamics
of Concepts and
Intellectual Suppression

Of relevance to the theme of change of understanding is the concept of the intellectual ideality. By its nature, a concept is ideal. What is meant by the ideality of thought is the impossibility of the full realization of the idea. When a concept is attempted to be realized, or to be brought to the domain of realization, a concept changes from its original form; it loses some of its content, depending on the conceptual change occurring as a result of being attempted to be realized in a social-cultural setting. Change of understanding with the change of circumstances of life cannot mean the full change of understanding or the full change of the circumstances of life. As social reality cannot always achieve the potential, it is impossible to have a full realization of the concept. Concepts, such as freedom, rationality, democracy, justice, equality, understanding, progress, imperative, reform change, for example, should they be manifested in a certain form, such a form is short of the full realization of such concepts. In the idea of the bravery of the knight and the generosity of the generous, for instance, is not embodied full bravery and full generosity. In the idea of the change of the understanding of the one who understands cannot be embodied the full change of understanding. They can be only partially realized. It is a gross injustice on the part of the human being to approach the partially realized concepts as fully realized. Such an approach entails grave implications in many fields. Not to give consideration to the impossibility of the full achievement of thought, or non-accommodation of the ideality of thought, involves intellectual suppression and fanaticism, as such lack of consideration results in the perception of a concept, in its use in the social context, as having been fully realized, whereas only a portion of its potential meaning was achieved.

Human concepts are not isolated from reality. They develop, in the sense that the human understanding of things changes with the change of circumstances which surround the human being. To look at a concept as an abstract intellectual form, coercively cut off from the active reality, is a look of a coercive extreme, as through such a view, the activities taking place through interaction between this view and reality are ignored. Human organizations, with their certain goals, should not be judged by the question whether or not they have realized a goal, but by the extent of its realization.

The relation of the abstract intellectual form to reality is less clear. In order for that relation to be clearer, that form should be embodied or reflected in the social reality.

Those who assume official and unofficial authority are those who decide, in the unfolding of form in that reality, their concept of the contents of that unfolding. In that, they do not adequately take into consideration the concepts of groups in which they have no interest.

What appears, on the abstract level, one intellectual form, turns out to be, at a level of less abstraction, different concepts, in view of the fact that the closer that abstract intellectual form is to practical reality, the presence of the subjective element in the human concept of the abstract intellectual form expands.

The preceding paragraphs show that human reality is an ever-aspiring reality; human society is one that is engaged in aspiring to achieve goals. The world, in a sense, is that which was partially realized of our goals. The world is not what we have aspired to; it is that measure of the partially realized goals.

Because of the constant interaction among concepts, and between them and the mind under changing cultural, economic, political and psychological circumstances in the passage of time in different locations, concepts in various fields have their dynamism; their contents are invariably changing. The content of the concept of "man" in the Islamic world differs from that of "man" in the West.

Because of the constant, though with a variable speed, change in the content of the seemingly same concepts, it is wrong to assume that there is a complete grasp or knowledge of a certain concept, in particular in cases where a concept is dealt with at a remote time distance.

It is erroneous that, when studying a given concept, such as a given phenomenon, to proceed from the belief that knowledge of that concept is complete, and that is because full knowledge is unachievable either because of the difficulty of its achievement or the continuity of the change of the concept's contents. Concept of family in the Islamic world is not that in the West.

Contents of concept vary depending on the extent of the presence of the objective dimension and of the ideological-subjective dimension of the cultural-political-economic circumstances. Content of the concept of "honor" with the Arabs and Muslims is not the content of that in the West. It is not easy to accurately identify concepts of modernity and modernization. In some societies, concept of modernity has become in the passage of time an ideological concept, and in some contexts, the concept, or perhaps aspects of it, became no longer neutral scientifically or objectively in as much as it is possible to achieve objectivity and scientific treatment. Aspects of this concept have become a mixture of subjective and objective aspects. Thus, this concept is not global. To facilitate achievement of advancement in the developing countries, and to scientifically study meanings of concepts such as mobility, progress, and awakening, it would be safer to avoid use of concepts that combine the objective with the subjective, such as modernity, and use concepts that are more objective such as development.

In view of the fact that the pattern of Western modernity stemmed from the Western social historical experience, it has characteristics stemming from the particularity of the Western experience. Hence, this pattern does not take into account the social historical characteristics of non-Western societies. In spite of that, scientific and objective technological aspects of Western modernity need to be utilized by the developing countries, in spite of the less friendly policies pursued by some Western countries towards issues of the developing countries.

At the less abstract level and the closer to the practical reality, the presence of the subjective element in the concept of those who assume authority is bigger, and their accommodation would be less or absent of the others' concept of the intellectual form.

It is necessary to know the dynamic nature of concepts in order to know the nature of social relations. It is impossible to generate descriptive, analytical, explanatory and predictive thought without having knowledge of this fundamental characteristic of concepts. Hence, it is impossible to know reality without knowing this characteristic.

Departing from the concept of the unity of natural phenomena and of the basic social phenomena, the intellectual split which exists in fields of human activity is an indication of the incompleteness of human knowledge and it is an important factor in preventing the attainment of a fuller knowledge of these phenomena.

In order to weaken the intellectual split or to eradicate it, it is necessary to adopt the concept of the dynamics of the social concepts as above stated. With this concept, there is no full independence for the educated person or for the career politician, or for the freedom of political or educational action, or for thorough criticism, or a full care for the public or private interest, or full backwardness or advancement. All of these are concepts of dynamic character. Given their dynamic character, they are relative concepts, relative to the strength of presence of the various intertwining and interactive components of a certain phenomenon, and of the presence of the various intertwining and interactive factors among themselves of other phenomena which have their changing impact on these components.

In the developing countries, and to a lesser extent in the developed countries, there are no educated people with independent thinking. This statement is made because independence or lack of it of intellectual independence of educated persons—and here we are talking about independence in its relative concept, as there is no full independence—is associated with the emergence of certain economic, political and social structures which allows a degree of freedom of expression, with no fear, of the critical independent view. Of these structures are emergence of civil society, laying and establishment of controls to be applied to official and unofficial political institutions. Civil society and those controls and checks are, to put it mildly, weak in the developing world. Consequently, educated people do not enjoy independence of critical thought.

This situation has hampered healthy development of society, because it is impossible for society to develop healthily without independence of thought and criticism, which are necessary to shed light on available alternatives of policy and action, and to make possible conduct of genuine dialogue among views for the interest of all.

Of the problems of thought is to consider two phenomena contradictory, and that is not because of contradiction between them, but because of inadequacy of human understanding. The reasons for this inadequacy, which are cultural, intellectual, value and psychological in nature, prevent the communication of the contents of a phenomenon to mind.

In the various cultural, economic and political fields one meaning is attributed to one concept. This kind of attribution is a kind of intellectual bigotry and intellectual suppression. Concept, which is a product of mind and thought, is a product of the various and varying historical, psychological and cultural circumstances. Concepts change with change of mind and thought. To say that concepts change does not mean that there is certain permanency in certain concepts such as those related to matters of belief. Attribution of one meaning to one concept involves ignorance of other meaning or meanings that must be attributed to that concept by virtue of the historicity of the human thought, in view of thought being influenced by prevailing socio-cultural-psychological circumstances.

In view of the fact that a number of aspects of the life of the developing peoples, including the political life, are still characterized with intellectual conservatism, and that such aspects are dominated by healthy and unhealthy traditions, given the fact that the patriarchal non-modern and non-democratic societies constitutes a suitable and fertile ground for persons with official and unofficial political interests to stay in positions of political authority, and in view of the fact that objective, independent and critical thought inescapably aims at changing or altering this situation, then it is natural that those with such interests would fight intellectual independence and independence of intellectual criticism and would act to marginalize and eliminate the role of the independent and critical educated and thinkers in society.

Ideologies and Intellectual Dichotomy

Ideological strictness helps bring about dichotomy. That is because strictness in adherence to something or strong affiliation with it would exclude the field that is not included in that adherence or affiliation. Thus, strictness in commitment to ideology involves exclusion of other ideological thought. This is true of phenomena such as dominant legends and mythologies. Given that strictness in commitment to ideological thought is narrower than the human reality, then that strictness is inescapably at the expense of the understanding of that reality.

For thousands of years interaction took place between mythology and ideology. Besides the values, principles, beliefs and suppositions with which people think and which people accept, they think with a group of tales and legendary stories. There is a mutual influence between beliefs and assumptions, on the one hand, and tales and legends, on the other. The social context is, to a certain extent, a mythological and ideological one. Domination of a part of those beliefs, assumptions, tales, legends and myths is likely to lead to extremism and dichotomy and bigotry.

Political and economic ideologies and tendencies, such as racial superiority and aggression, are forms of intellectual dichotomy and, consequently, intellectual suppression. Given that dichotomy is being limited and restricted by one thought only, it is an intellectual inertia, intellectual impenetrability, ideological restriction and intellectual unilateralism. Given the fact that dichotomy is a complete alignment with a certain view, it excludes any other view. Racism aligns itself with one party or side, excluding and rejecting other parties or views. Intellectual bigotry and suppression are reflected in Nazism and other racist ideologies, even though they may be dressed with a humanitarian garment, which exclude the right of basic equality among humans.

Religious sectarianism, which involves making religious affiliation the only or decisive factor in the allocation of senior political, financial, managerial and military posts in the state or province, does involve intellectual suppression. This is because it does not allow other factors to play a role in determining that allocation, even though such factors may be a source of benefit for the state bigger than that which the state derives from the determination by the religious affiliation of that allocation.

By excluding the right of equality among people through a doctrine of alleged and mythical racial superiority, Nazism is a suppressive line of thinking. There are no really objective and serious studies that prove that the Aryan race is superior to non-Aryan races in terms of understanding or intelligence. The European peoples were in the Middle Ages passing through certain political, social and cultural conditions, some of which—such as the search for democratization—are being experienced today by the peoples of the developing countries. Hundreds of millions of Westerners do not know the extent of the intelligence of the peoples of the developing world and do not know the extent of their own fallacies in certain fields, when it comes to matters affecting their lives domestically and outside their countries.

Inherent in the claim to play a civilizing role in the non-Western world or to carry the burden of spreading civilization is intellectual suppression, as by this claim it is clearly implied that non-Western peoples lack culture and that Western culture is better and superior than non-Western culture. To state that Western culture needs to be adopted in order to rescue peoples from their current conditions means that these peoples have no cultures, and that their cultures are inadequate and are placed in an inferior position vis-à-vis the Western culture.

Additionally, intellectual suppression in the line of thinking called communism is probably reflected in the exclusion of forces, other than the economic factor, that influence human history, and, more specifically, the identity of those who own the means of production. The movement of human history is not explained only by this factor, in spite of its importance. Besides this factor, the course of history is explainable by such factors as sexual drive, culture, belief, psychology and mythology.

Each social context contains an ideological element. One of the functions of the adoption of a certain ideology may be perpetuation of the existing social-political system. It is inescapable that such a system is based on disparity in the allocation of the social and economic benefits. Those who benefit from the adoption of a certain ideology would refuse to eliminate or reduce the effect of such an ideology. Because of the consideration of such benefit, the effect of objectivity and of analysis in contexts in which ideology constitutes an important factor is reduced. Hence, it is incorrect to claim pursuit of objectivity in a social context. Such a claim would carry the meaning of an attempt to influence the ideology of those to whom such a claim is addressed. In spite of the impossibility of the full removal of ideology in social life, it may be possible, in an environment dominated by ideology, to reach only a part of the objective truth. As mythology, which has a strong element of ideology, is usually lacking in objective thinking, it is limited. Mythological structure of thought hides, to various degrees, the natural and human reality. When facing the reality on the ground, the irrelevance of such structure to reality becomes clearer. As this thought is narrower than reality, adoption of this thinking is bound to be at the expense of the understanding of reality.

Names and Slowness of Intellectual Development

A name does not always indicate that which is named. The indication of what is named is not identical sometimes with the meaning to which the name refers, because of change continuously occurring in the meaning of the name given the dynamism of the interactive dimensions of the complex and active political, social, cultural and psychological reality. Given this changing reality, names acquire meanings which were assumed that such names were not containing and that were initially assumed that they were contained in other names. Meanings are attributed to a name while, as a result of the interaction of the dimensions of reality imbued with change, such a name is devoid of such meanings, and meanings are not attributed to a certain name whereas such a name became, because of that reality, containing such meanings. In other words, such changes occur in the meanings of names without change of such names in order to fit with changes in the meanings of names. Capitalism, socialism, democracy, and republican and royal regimes, for example, have meanings which, to a certain extent, differ from their meanings in the past. In spite of that, the formulation of names for such named things remains the same. This also contributes to explain that services of social welfare, health insurance and social security in some countries, even though named capitalistic, are more developed and in more practice than those in republican countries, and that concentration of political authority in some socialistic countries was stronger than that in some capitalistic countries. This also contributes to explaining the fact that some beliefs and practices, such as search for employment opportunities, improvement of status of women, raising the level of living, spread of learning, elimination of poverty and establishment of universities are shared by different intellectual and social currents.

Dichotomy, Analysis and Explanation

Explanation, which theorization involves, is establishment of causal relations between phenomena. Explanation would be inadequate if it does not include all the relevant phenomena. In spite of some benefit drawn from analysis as one of the tools of knowing the cause and effect, it has a shortcoming theoretically and practically. Analysis has a theoretical shortcoming because through it one cannot have a full knowledge of reality because reality is wider than it could be known through intellectual formulations alleging they have uncovered the relation between cause and effect. Analysis has a practical shortcoming because the analyst's social and psychological background makes him selective, to a certain extent, when analyzing. The wide and comprehensive reality by nature would not be known by a means which is not wide and not comprehensive, namely, the means of selective analysis.

A major flaw in many of the writings and utterances in the field of social sciences, including those theoretical and philosophical writings by Western thinkers, is the tendency to explain a social phenomenon, which has a complex and dynamic nature, by one factor or to attribute it to one factor, whereas explanation of a social phenomenon, because of its complex and dynamic nature, requires taking into account all the relevant factors, including multitude of dimensions of the origin of a phenomenon vertically, that is to say, change of impact of circumstances as a result of the passage of times on the strength of factors that bring about human behavior and attitudes, and horizontally, that is to say, multitude of factors that create a phenomenon, and taking into account complexity of the human individual, which is embodied in the multitude of dimensions, and dynamism of this multitude and of the individual embodied in the continuing interaction among these dimensions.

Non-explanation of a phenomenon by all the factors comes at the expense of the other factors in the emergence of the phenomenon, thus this kind of explanation does ignore those factors, doing injustice to them, and defacing their presence and effects.

This way of explaining is intellectually dichotomous. Social phenomena cannot be comprehensively explained unless they are considered as resulting not from one factor, but from a multitude of factors. Being complex and dynamic, a social phenomenon is explainable by more than one factor. Explanation of a phenomenon with one factor indicates deficiency and inadequacy in explanation.

Explanation of a phenomenon with only one factor is extremism in being sensitive to that factor at the expense of the other factors.

Inadequate explanation, namely explanation which does take only one factor in the emergence of a phenomenon, is a domineering and transgressive uniform line of thinking, in the sense that the above factor is mistakenly regarded as domineering over the other ignored, though present, factors.

By ascribing a phenomenon to one factor, other factors are excluded. Being unmindful of other factors, this type of explanation is less than open-minded. Hampering dialogue between the acknowledged factor or factors and the excluded factors, this type of explanation militates against the smooth flow of communication. By recognizing, and satisfying one's self with, one factor, recognition of the presence of other factors is suppressed.

Thus, it is incorrect to attribute human behavior to the sexual drive only, or to the incentive to earning and accumulation of material wealth only. Nor is it correct to attribute human history to one factor only, that of the identity of those who control or own the means of production. Explanation of human behavior by the sexual drive embodies intellectual suppression because such explanation suppresses factors other than the sexual factor in explaining the human behavior. The same applies to explaining human history by the identity of those who control or own means of production. It is also incorrect to explain human behavior with the incentive to acquire and accumulate material wealth only. It is also wrong to limit explaining the political Arab behavior to a nationalist, economic or religious factor or the factor of the social legacy. It is also wrong to restrict the explanation of behavior of states to only foreign factors or internal factors.

The current case of some Arab peoples, which is characterized by weakness, poverty, cannot be explained with only one factor. This case needs to be explained with a multitude of factors, including the length of foreign rule, imperialism, settlement, Western expansion, foreign hegemony, disagreement among the Arab states, inadequate development of Arab political awareness, sectarianism, romanticism, inferiority of the status of women, weakness of its legal status, France's and Britain's partition of the Arab lands which were part of the Ottoman Sultanate, Arab exposure to foreign threats before they were able to unite their positions and to be committed to a form of unification. Of these factors also, excess in the adoption of the capitalistic system, despotism, lack of establishing of social justice, lack of upbringing on independent thinking, domination of the patriarchal rule, prevention of Arab countries and peoples from political and economic form of unification. An example of that is France's and Britain's prevention of Muhammad 'Ali, ruler of Egypt in the 19th century, from unifying Egypt, Syria and other Arab countries. Of these factors also are corruption, bribery, partiality, and the weakness of the "state" as such, weakness of individualism and excess in it at the same time, and emphasis on conformism.

Exclusion of relevant factors from the explanation of social phenomena has slowed down and continues to slow down the advance of social sciences.

No two informed persons disagree that the problems from which Arabs and Muslims are suffering from in various fields are explainable by the influence of both external and internal factors in spite of the difference among analysts in determining the extent of the influence exerted by each of these factors. This difference is attributable to the difficulty in drawing clear boundaries between the external and internal factors. The main reason of this difficulty is the difficulty in determining the beginning and end of influence at the horizontal (geographic) level and the vertical (historical) level. The source of this difficulty is also the interaction that takes place between the external and internal factors, an interaction that leads to dynamism of relations between them. Given the continuous mutual influence between them, there would certainly emerge common zones between them.

In the passage of time, factors in the emergence of a phenomenon undergo change, and the extent of the presence or effect of each of these factors also changes as a result of the continuing change of the social, cultural, economic and psychological circumstances and of the continuing interaction between those circumstances and the phenomenon and the individual, in the sense that one's personality does also comprise of constantly interactive subjective and objective elements. The longer is the time, the stronger is the influence of interactions among all the circumstances and factors.

Restriction of explanation of a social phenomenon to one factor involves extremism and bigotry. This restriction excludes other factors that are needed to complete explanation, such as the ethical and religious dimension. This method of explanation has and continues to slow down the advance of social sciences and has negatively affected thought of those who adopted it.

What delays increase of human knowledge is human tendency to explain all phenomena in the time and geographical space of the universe with familiar patterns of the sole field which we know from our direct experiences. This explanation is limited by the limitedness of the familiar patterns of people. Satisfaction with this explanation comes at the expense of our acquiring knowledge of unknown patterns.

With adopting a certain line of uniform thinking, a certain method, approach or consideration implicit in that uniform line of thinking is accommodated, and other approaches are ignored, in spite of those approaches presence in the phenomenon and in the circumstances and factors that are giving rise to such phenomenon or affecting it.

A manifestation of dichotomy is that a party attributes an entire human achievement to it and that it does not attribute a portion of that achievement to other parties. Some Western actors have a tendency to deny non-Western peoples playing a role in the emergence and development of civilizations. Some Western attempts have been made to deface non-Western civilization influence on the Western civilization. This extremism is seen in statements by some Western actors that creators of civilization are restricted to Europeans and their descendants.

These statements are not correct. Europe has not been the only source of scientific and technological civilization. This civilization is the product of human development which lasted for centuries. Not only Europeans in the last two centuries, but also ancient Egyptians, Assyrians, Canaanites, Phoenicians, Chinese, Indian, Muslims and Arabs an important role in the creation and development of civilization. A number of modern European inventions are based on scientific theories which were discovered by scholars in Asia and Africa in the Medieval Ages. Arabic, with its grammar, syntax, and rules governing use of its verbs and nouns is a great civilization achievement by any criterion

In the saying that conflict of civilizations is the only factor that explains human history is involved an intellectual suppression, as such conception involves exclusion of other factors that have contributed to human history. Study of the rise and development of civilizations has revealed civilization interaction on the inter-continental level.

Determinism and Selectivity

Some of the reasons of determinism and selectivity, which are a uniform line of thinking, are the presence of the subjective and objective factors in peoples' propositions, inadequacy of understanding, negligence of the scientific approach, upbringing on deterministic and selective ways of addressing matters, and ignorance of more precise articulation of ideas. Determinism and selectivity corrupt the consistent and the intellectually, scientifically and philosophically organized propositions. This line of thinking, being dichotomous, obstructs coherent presentation. Through such proposition, subjective and ideological points that have no relevance to such proposition are excluded. An additional reason is the inability by those who make statements to put forward consistent scientific and theoretical propositions, or their lack of appreciation of such propositions. A further reason is the exponent's fear that he would be misunderstood if, in his statement, he pursued scientific and intellectual consistency. In determinism inheres the exclusion of what is not taken account of. Selectivity implies the existence of things that have not been selected. Thus, both determinism and selectivity are restrictive, exclusivist and suppressive, because through them one excludes aspects of relevance to the objective. Both involve lack of openness on the probability of the error the determining one is committing.

Given the fact that one who has tendency to determinism is exaggerating in his self-confidence, he is shallow-minded. They militate against open-mindedness and interaction. To attribute full responsibility for the emergence of certain phenomena to some factors, to the exclusion of others, are sorts of selectivity and determinism. Selectivity and determinism have manifested and still manifest themselves in all cultures. They are drawbacks affecting the lines of thought of a considerable number of writers in all parts of the world. They imply absolute acceptance of certain ideas. Involving acceptance of some ideas and exclusion of others, they do not allow for dialogue and are contrary to open-mindedness. Having acceptance limited to one line of thought, they are dichotomous. Often, the tone of determinism and selectivity is sharp and unsubstantiated.

Some examples of this selectivity are that some people attribute full responsibility for the Arab's miserable conditions to only the Arab culture, whereas others confine the full responsibility to foreign rule, and that some people attribute full responsibility for the poverty in the developing countries to only the governing authorities, whereas others consider this poverty only the result of the lack of adequate initiative on the part of these countries.

In fact, there is always more than one factor responsible for a certain phenomenon. In the Arab case, for example, unhealthy Arab upbringing, Arab romanticism, sectarianism, patriarchal system, foreign rule, a legacy of political oppression and other reasons are responsible for the Arab social and political underdevelopment.

Selectivity is inappropriate as it does not help in seeing the whole picture of a certain condition. This condition cannot be adequately treated without knowing all of the reasons for its emergence. To treat only a part of the reasons is not enough, because the unselected, and hence untreated, reasons would vitiate the effect of the treatment of the selected reasons.

Excessive Capitalism
and Rationalism

Uniform lines of thinking have also taken on the form of excessive capitalism and the over-emphasis on rationalism in certain fields of thought and practice. Intellectual suppression in excessive capitalism is reflected in the exclusion of currents that, though adopting capitalism, do stress accommodation of considerations as to how wealth is distributed, how the benefit to all population strata is secured and how the gap between the few wealthy and the many poor is narrowed—acknowledging that that benefit is various and varying—at the level of a country's economic system and at the international level.

In the Western model of modernity there is excess of stress on what Western modernists call "rationalism." Some analysts mean by rationalism solution of problems, through rational means, which humanity has and is facing. Over-emphasis on rationalism has received a fair amount of criticism. Such model of modernity ignores, to a certain extent, the non-rational aspect in the human being and in his cultural and spiritual experience, leading to failure of solution of many problems and to the creation of other problems. Excessive rationalism comes, to varying degrees, at the expense of the spiritual and human dimension in the lives of people and their social relations at the state and world levels. Intellectual suppression in the excess of rationalism is reflected in the exaggerated importance given in this trend to the rationalistic approach to the solution of complex human conditions. Thought with excessive rationalism does not penetrate into the micro-details of real human situations in which various and many human and cultural dimensions are manifested.

This line of thinking has led to the exclusion or weakening of the humanistic dimension in the individual and his/her behavior and to excessive individualism and excessive materialism, and to the very strong sense of alienation and exile socially, emotionally and intellectually.

Excessive emphasis on rationalism has another suppressive aspect. This emphasis led to excesses in organization. Such organizational excesses do not take into account the social and humanistic characteristics in the human life. Such excesses involve phenomena such as extremism, fanaticism, bigotry and narrow mindedness, such as Nazism, fascism, worship of one certain intellectual idol and legalistic approach of human relations.

Such excesses in organization involve excess in the emphasis of concepts such as effectiveness, efficiency, and enchantment with certain ideas, so much so that one becomes captivated by them. Excessive effectiveness tends to passively affect the human needs. Excesses in such concepts come at the expense of the humanity of the human being and human relations. They cause excess in the emphasis on the importance of science and technology, contributing to placing science and technology in a center which comes at the expense of the psychological, human and spiritual aspect of man, and on the too legalistic interpretation and reading of human conditions, that legal and legalistic interpretation cannot fathom and that is indifferent to the understanding and accommodation of such conditions.

Given the fact that understanding of the nature of relations between individuals, groups and states is possible only through explanation that takes into account the intellectual, humanistic and spiritual dimensions of such relations, then such line of thinking has considerably slowed down and are still slowing down the progress of social sciences.

Excessively rationalistic thought does not reach the micro-details of reality in which, in many situations, human, humanistic and spiritual dimensions are reflected. Hence, excess in rationalistic tendency suppress such a dimension.

Given that it is impossible to understand the nature of relations between individuals, groups and states without explanation that takes into account the mental, humanistic and spiritual dimensions of such relations, uniform lines of thinking slowed down and continue considerably to slow down progress of the social and humanistic sciences.

Hierarchical Order and Intellectual Transgression

Even though the scope of human knowledge has widened considerably, truths have not yet been discovered. Frequently, people pass judgments that are not based on knowledge; many of these judgments touch on aspects of things unknown. This means transgression, sometimes, of thought on what is not known. It is a haughty and defiant human tendency to enter domains on which the human being is not qualified to pass judgment.

It occurs to people all over the world that each one's thought is dominated by a certain idea or a group of ideas. Such domination, which means exclusion or marginalization of the non-dominant ideas, creates an intellectual imbalance, as there is no equal intellectual share of attention to ideas. Such domination involves suppression, as the non-dominating ideas exist in the shadow of the dominant ones.

Often categorical rule contains extremism in the taking of position and suppression. With exception to belief and transcendental aspects and statements that rely on objective and tangible truths, it is incorrect for one to believe in the certainty of his propositions. With unjustified intellectual certainty, aspects which that person is not aware that he is not aware of or which are not covered by the field of his categorical or certain thought are defaced. What is so dangerous is for one to be restricted by the acceptance of an idea and to be its captive and slave.

Hierarchical social system, which is in existence in all human societies, has a very strong suppressive influence. There are many aspects of human life which are not accommodated by the hierarchical system. Such a system suppresses a lot of what is contradictory with the requirements of the hierarchical system. As the requirements of such a system are not necessarily matching with the contributions of thinkers, literary figures and artists, then such a system does not accommodate at least some of these contributions.

Existential Dynamism
and Open Mindedness

Existence contains human and natural dimensions. Human existence, which includes individuals, groups, societies, peoples, states, political and economic relations, psychological influences, historical legacies, conceptions, ideas and beliefs, is dynamic. Being dynamic, they are in constant mutual influence. Continued mutual influence between the human and natural dimensions with their various components tends to change the circumstances, with attendant change of intellectual impenetrability. Speed of change varies depending on the extent of presence of the natural and human dimensions in the context. Thus, change may be slow and is difficult to discern.

Intellectual conservatism does not go hand in hand with openness, creativity and roaming space in the intellectual field. That is because intellectual conservatism has no strong tendency to intellectual taking-off, unleashed intellectual imagination and penetrating into the deep intellectual space. Intellectual conservatism seeks, by its nature, to conserve the existing thought, whereas in the nature of openness, emancipation and creativity in the intellectual space is inherent a tendency to intellectual renewal and to change what needs to be changed of the existing thought.

One of the features of progress is intellectual openness to the various domains of life and the cosmos, and the psychological and intellectual willingness to have dialogue with such domains. Measurement of progress is the extent of such open-mindedness. This open-mindedness would be achieved through awareness of the dynamism of concepts. One of the tools to promote such awareness is intellectual, mental and philosophical criticism and logical and mathematical thought. Hence, progress means the availability of the intellectual ability to handle the human problematic conditions which prevent humanity from diagnosing human illnesses and proceed forward with life and existence.

An indication of awareness would be the willingness to deal rationally and objectively with reality and its requirements. This would not be possible without realization of the political and social intellectual freedom: freedom of the individual in his decision and his choice and actions, of course within the high values adopted and pursued by the society and its interests. This intellectual freedom is the main tributary of intellectual creativity. Realization of freedom means realization of the potential of creativity.

Intellectual openness is important to achieve change and development, as through intellectual openness intellectual interaction is achieved, thus avoiding stagnation and promoting change and development.

Intellectual openness has to do with cultural openness. Intellectual openness promotes cultural openness and, consequently, cultural interaction. Through intellectual interaction, one's intellectual and cultural identity is not necessarily lost, but it is altered.

Intellectual openness, which contradicts intellectual impenetrability, may weaken or remove intellectual bigotry. Mental habit is one factor of intellectual impenetrability or intellectual openness. A proof of intellectual inertia is to have one's behavior within the circle of the limited and restricted intellectual imagination, and not traveling in its relations to the social environment beyond the known and familiar thought.

In order for thought to be open-minded, it must be interactive with the intellectual and social environments in the broadest sense of the word. In order for thought to be described as interactive, it must be open-minded. If it is not open-minded, it is not interactive. Open-mindedness negates closure and impenetrability, which negate interaction. Interaction implies that one of the features of thought is that it proceeds from the assumption of the insufficiency of knowledge and from the assumption that human knowledge is not complete, and that increase in knowledge through interaction is psychologically satisfying process and rewarding scientifically and socially. Interaction also implies that one of the features of thought is that it proceeds from the psychological and intellectual readiness to not to reject the new just because it is new and because it does not fall into the domain of knowledge.

Dogmatism and intellectual immobility, which are a kind of intellectual dichotomy, negate open mindedness, which is needed intellectual interaction. Through criticism, which is dynamic, intellectual weakness of dogmatism and intellectual immobility are uncovered. Through criticism, humans can adjust themselves to world's facts and realities.

Passing of Judgment, Generalization and Suppression

Passing of judgment, without adequate study of the case, on any people, involves ignorance and suppression of the national and international social, cultural, psychological and historical circumstances which have their influence on reality and the creation of reality. Passing of judgment involves suppression and dichotomy, because with such judgment, there would be an element of ignoring and defacing certain existing truths, and there would be a subjective factor which is given undeserved weight against the objective reality.

It is sound intellectually and socially to reflect before passing a judgment on whatever social phenomena. Pondering would be reflected in conduct of a serious study before passing judgment on them. Self-deterrence from passing a judgment without pondering—driven by one's knowledge of the error involved in hastening to pass a judgment—would indicate an availability of a more considerable amount of intellectual maturity. It is more likely that the share of the subjective motives is bigger in the judgment that was passed without pondering, and that the share of the objective motives is bigger in the judgment after ample study.

To place the full responsibility, for instance, for the slow cultural-economic development in the developing countries on domestic factors is wrong. Besides these factors in this case, there are important foreign factors. It is not easy for the developing peoples to digest in a relatively short time Western cultural aspects whose development took centuries. Even though some of these aspects were felt in the Ottoman State, which included Arab lands, the impact of such aspects, though important, was limited.

The length of the time of adoption and development in the field of modernity in the West has alleviated the impact of such adoption and development on the people. It was but natural that that development was cumulative, thus decreasing the effect of such change.

Unverified or unascertained generalization does not merit to be called generalization. Being a statement with absolute terms, generalization is a frozen uniform line of thinking. Generalization is described as frozen because its intellectual statement is a statement which is limited to that which is covered by the generalization, inattentive to what was not covered with generalization. It is described as a restrictive thought because it restricts one's intellectual point of proceeding. It is described as oppressive because it ignores the existence of other ideas that are not included in the frame of that generalization. It is described as exclusivist because one, with generalization, excludes what is not included within that generalization. Generalization rejects to include within its frame phenomena and ideas that generalization excludes. Given that generalization is a contradictory intellectual extreme, then its intellectual behavior is restricted and restrictive. To say that rural people are backward means that no adjective of progress was attributed to them. This is erroneous in terms of the manner of treatment and from the perspective of reality also.

By the same token, it is erroneous to say that the European society is advanced and that societies of the developing countries are backward; that boy is superior and girl is inferior mentally and intellectually: that Arabs or any other people are fully advanced or fully backward. It is also wrong to say that nationalism is predicated on only one factor, or that the difficult Arab state of affairs is attributable to one foreign factor only, or that it is attributable only on an economic, historical, value-based, geographical, political, or psychological factor. It is also wrong to say that material or money is the only criterion for happiness, and that life would only be explained by science. Given that that thinking is bigot dichotomous, it is deficient; it is thought that does not understand reality nor does it know how to address issues that need examination.

One of such generalizations is the statement that there is no original thought on the part of some peoples. As a matter of fact, each people must have an original thought. A people's life in special circumstances requires that those people produce original thought which enables them to live in those circumstances, and to articulate, at the same time, the special life conditions lived by those people.

Moreover, an indication of the wrong in the statement that some peoples have no original thought is that each people have more than one general intellectual structure. Whereas some structures are visible, others are invisible, hidden or suppressed. To say that a people have no original thought on the basis of visible structure, ignoring other hidden structures of original thought, is an act of oppression, which is prohibited by principles of justice, fairness and logic.

In any human society, there are multiple factors in concealing the intellectual structures or in their exclusion, elimination, suppression or negligence. Such and similar factors are caused by political suppression, governmental despotism, intellectual terrorism, psychological setup and constraint, and other factors. Should these structures have not been in existence, concealment of intellectual structures would not have occurred, and intellectual structures other than that known structure would have emerged, and those structures or others would have replaced that known structure. In addition to the written or read intellectual structures, there are also verbal intellectual structures.

To make general conclusions on the basis of limited and biased observations is a kind of generalization. With these conclusions, which limit increase of human knowledge, sources of data which are there but which we are not aware of are ignored. What is relevant for this human tendency to conclusions is the thinking embodied in the saying that man is the criterion of all things. It is sound to say that man is a criterion for all perceived things. With the spread of that former thinking we should not be surprised from peoples' having their imprint on nearly every evaluation.

Given the substantive and methodological drawback which is involved in extremism and bigotry and given the relativity of perceived and non-transcendental things and the error of absolute or generalized thinking, it is sound that the human being avoid use of expressions of extreme thinking or wording which expresses bigot thought in cases where make avoidance of their use necessary such as the phrase "except to," and "only." En example of such use is "only a man can awake these people" and "on the surface of the earth there is nothing except evil."

By the same token, it would be sound to use expressions which do not encourage or indicate intellectual extremism and which, rather, encourage and indicate intellectual pluralism. Of such expressions are the following: "of these factors are factors . . . ,"; "I would not be far from truth if I say . . . ," Of what has emerged from the statement is . . . ," and "of the ideas contained in the report . . ."

The healthier and the less deficient mind is that which does not tend, with its existing deficiency and value biases, to pass economic, historical, social or cultural generalizations.

The human self has its wishes, positions and ways of behavior which interact with each other. The human self is influenced by the different circumstances which are changing with the passage of time. These qualities of the self, the intellectual and ideological differences and contrasts, the social and cultural changes, changes of positions and moods and the continuous interaction between these and other factors make it erroneous intellectually and mentally to pass generalizations.

The lack of revealing of the existence of things is a factor in the defacement of existing intellectual structures, because emergence of intellectual structure is attributable to each of the known and hidden things. Political and intellectual suppression and social suppression, official and unofficial despotism, psychological composition, foreign rule, sectionalism, tribalism, feudalism injustice, and arbitrariness are things that determine the nature of intellectual structures. They themselves may be and it is highly likely that a part of them are hidden or invisible. These and other factors have a significant impact in exclusion, suppression, negligence and marginalization in the intellectual and social sphere. Had these undisclosed factors not existed, the familiar structure would not have emerged, and other intellectual structures would have emerged.

Lack of attention to discovering things unknown leaves impact on the nature of the position of the human being. One's lack of knowledge of unknown things makes him tend to pay a greater attention which is disproportionate to what he knows, and to stick in some cases to what he knows, in spite of the intellectual dilemma caused by restricting attention to what is known, and to rush, in some cases, to pass generalizations on what he does not know. Hence, there is the need to reveal things to achieve a smaller amount of imbalance in passing judgment and generalizations.

It also needs to be noted that mind is not the only source of knowledge. Two other sources are intuition and faith. There are domains which we can know about not through mind, but through intuition and faith.

In order for the human being to be able to remove problems that are besieging him, he should look for his own truth. He should not cease this search. Knowledge is the first step on the road leading to know the truth of things. Knowledge, resulting from mind, intuition and faith, is the source of freedom and emancipation.

A human being who has not discovered the human truth is not a real, genuine human individual. In order for the human being to be fully devoted, he should believe in himself, and he cannot believe in himself without knowing his essential truth.

Being dialectically related, a dynamic influence exists between the past and the present. To exclude the past's influence on the present, or the present's influence on the past would be suppression of the presence of the excluded factor.

When talked about a mutual influence between the past and the present, it is not meant that the amount of such an influence is equal.

As the writer's circumstances have a say in his/her position towards the past, and as the past has an influence on the writer's circumstances, it is wrong to say that the past dominates, or vice versa. Even those calling for return to the past, launch this call while influenced by the present's circumstances which have a say in determining the position taken towards the past.

Survival of the Fittest
and Suppression

Somewhat related to the alleged message of the spread of civilization is the suppressive idea of the survival of the fittest. This idea has some currency in the West. Is involves the domination of the strong actor, whether it is a state, company or organization, over a weak state or people politically, militarily, economically and culturally. This idea excludes the right of the vulnerable from the mentioned aspects. It may be the apex of the negligence of the human dimension: Who promotes this idea perhaps lacks a sense of human balance. In practical terms, how could members of a tribe that lack knowledge and live amidst forests survive and stand out vis-à-vis the educated, trained and well-armed man? Such members are very vulnerable.

Exponents of the idea of the survival of the fittest are morally wrong to claim that such people, who lack the ability to protect themselves, are not fitted for survival and that, accordingly, must be decimated. The suppressive aspect of such a claim is that it regards might as the only attribute for survival; it confines the fitness for survival to force, whereas fitness for survival can be achieved by means other than force, such as common affiliation to humanity, habitation on mother Earth, common ultimate and imperative physical end of the human being, common sharing of the basic biological and emotional human needs, and common fear of the wrath of nature. Is the price that should be paid by a state that lacks knowledge and modern science and technology to cease to exist, or to be dominated and destroyed by a stronger state or company whose personnel are educated, trained and experts? Must the vulnerable population in that state be perished because of their inability to protect themselves from the stronger man or state?

The idea of the survival of the fittest has historical roots in Europe. It was exposed and adopted by European thinkers and rulers in the medieval times, when European exploration and expansion needed a theoretical formulation to serve as an intellectual and ideological basis for such expansion. It would be useful to state the historical background for the adoption of such an idea in Europe. Adoption of this idea at the present time may be due to ignorance of its historical colonial and ideological roots or in order to serve as an ideological and political tool in the hands of those who adopt it now.

The attitude of exponents of this idea at the present time might be affected by their knowing the historical, colonial and ideological background of such an idea. To adopt such a line of thinking these days, without knowledge of its historical background and without the objective of serving a political and ideological agenda nowadays, would be suppressive by forcing ideological and intellectual formulation that was adopted long ago into present-day reality with its different needs.

Intellectual suppression in the uniform line of thinking is reflected in explain history with one factor, such as the factor of sex, cultural affiliation, psychology or economy. The doctrine of survival for the fittest, which is spread mainly in the West, involves intellectual extremism and the idea of the right of economically, bodily, economically or militarily stronger party in survival; it involves the idea of hegemony of the strong party, be it a state or organization, over a weak state, people, or a group. This hegemony or lack of survival seems to be the price that needs to be paid by state which lacks to knowledge, modern science and technology. Should these vulnerable people perish because of their inability to protect themselves from the stronger man, organization or state? This idea excludes right from the vulnerable people. This idea may be the peak of barbarity and of the negligence of the human dimension. He who promotes this idea lacks in sense of humanity.

Subjective and Objective
Factors and Prestige

In human society, aspects of factors, such as cultural, political, economic, psychological, are neutral, in the sense that they lend themselves to be utilized, in a state or society, regardless of its type of social order, political structure or cultural-political orientation. It is the content of policy, or value orientation of a given social organization, or the socio-political vision or a value system which determines the type or nature of role these factors perform. Factors, such as learning or taking initiative, can support certain regimes, such as dictatorship, democracy or autocracy. Wealth owned by certain people can be put to use for establishing justice, for production of weapons, for decimating people or for opening a dance bar.

Because of the complexity of the dynamic interactive social-psychological phenomena, more than one factor plays a role in the creation of a social—including political, cultural, psychological and historical—phenomenon. Hence, this phenomenon cannot be explained by one factor only. These factors, however, vary in terms of their presence or influence in the creation of such phenomena. That factors vary in their influence does not mean that a factor with a lesser influence could be dismissed, as a factor with bigger or lesser influence at a certain time can change the size of its influence in some other time.

Because phenomena are dynamic, they are changing. Because phenomena are dynamic and changing, they do not accept to be covered by a certain generalization, given that generalization is frozen. Frozen generalization does not qualify to cover or include changing phenomena. Adherence to generalization with regard to constant change involves social and cultural intellectual suppression.

By the same token, the attribution to any social phenomenon of internal factors only or external factors only is inherently divisive and involves intellectual suppression. This attribution suppresses the factors that are excluded. For example, the social, political, cultural, psychological and national crisis that the Arabs, Africans or any people are facing is attributable to, and, hence, explainable by, both internal and external factors.

Prestige or sense of prestige is a source of enjoyment for the human being. One who has prestige enjoys having it. It is a source of satisfaction for him because it strengthens his ego. Because prestige is a tool to generate and exercise economic and political influence, one who has it attaches to it great importance. And because one who has prestige knows its importance in acquiring influence and because he enjoys it, he always tries to keep, protect and promote it. The stronger is the prestige, the greater is its enjoyment, and the greater is the care to maintain and promote it.

One's prestige is based on objective factors or bases, such as professionalism or craft, and subjective factors or bases, such as giving respect to the elderly, or prestige which people attribute to one who is descendant, or he claims he is descendant, from privileged family, or from the class of notables, and the attribution of extraordinary acts to certain persons. The fact is that the subjective factor is forced onto the objective factor.

Objective and subjective bases differ one from the other in the extent of their presence or proportion in the source of prestige. Extent of this difference depends on factors, some of which are the extent of the social, political and technological development achieved by the people, extent of the people's absorption of professional and scientific values, the extent of the entrenchment and domination of the patriarchal system, extent of the prevalence of upbringing on the values of freedom, democracy and human dignity, extent of respect for, and pursuit of, the scientific and experimental approach. Presence of the subjective bases in the source of prestige is a main reason for the underdevelopment from which many people are suffering in the various socio-cultural fields.

The objective factor is not independent of the subjective factor in many concepts such as stability, liberation, achievements of order, criticism, contentment and status. What is meant by the objective factor is the factor that the nature of the subject requires its (the factor's) accommodation, and what is meant by the subjective factor is one that is not related to the objective factor. It is probably impossible to fully separate between the objective and subjective factors in social concepts. The lower is one's intellectual and educational level the more difficult is on average for him to separate between the subjective and objective factors. This lack or inadequacy of distinction is one of the main reasons for the educational, scientific and economic underdevelopment of peoples.

In order for one to strengthen the objective element in his thinking, he should keep a distance between himself and the theme of his thought. As long as one is aware of this distance and accommodating to it, the presence of the subjective in his thought would likely to diminish and the presence of the objective would likely to increase. Lack of separation between the self and the object in thought would be at the expense of knowledge of the object and of reality, and would be a marginalization of the human awareness of their existence.

One has a tendency to streamline the subjective factor over the objective factor if his sense of his prestige depends more on the subjective factor than on the objective factor.

Because of difference between the subjective factor and the objective factor, a contrast arises between them in the self of one who has sense of prestige in socio-economic contexts. Within one who has this sense, either the objective factor or the subjective factor is dominant. The following is an example drawn from field of development on such a contradiction: objectively, socio-economic development requires availability of a significant amount of participation by people in the process of development. It is inescapable that achievement of development involves people's participation. However, one who assumes authority—for instance, a ruler, minister, mayor, village head, police officer, commander of an army or director—may take, from starting point of his desire to keep his prestige, a cautious, hesitant, indifferent, reluctant or hostile position towards the idea of popular participation. He might think that accommodation of such participation does not fit his exercise of authority which forms, from his viewpoint and the viewpoint of others, one of his strong bases of his prestige. It is clear that this position would be one important reason for preventing or slowing down development.

Related to the achievement of desired development is the matter of individualism. In the world, mainly the developing world, "individualism" is not sufficiently developed. "Individualism" in these countries is affected by a number of institutions such as family and clan affiliation, tribalism, factionalism, excessive prohibitions and prescriptions on the human person, totalitarianism, autocracy, strong state mechanisms and organs.

These institutions have slowed down or hindered the development of an individual.

Under these circumstances, the person, to a far extent, is not recognized or identified as an individual. He is understood and regarded as a harnessed and adjunct person. To a far extent, his existence acquires its meaning through his affixation to a family, tribe, class, sect or faction. Mainly, these are the criteria according to which a person's standing is determined by the rest.

Thus, person loses his essential value as an individual. In this situation he may be likened to a tool, or to a commodity. Instead of being looked at as an existing entity in himself, he is looked at as a part of something. Thus, his identity as an individual is ignored or suppressed. Relations to him are predicated on the view that he is a part of a larger group.

The human individual can play not only an important, but also a leading, role in causing change to happen. Desired change can be caused by the synchronized actions of various factors, one of which is the action or role played by the individual with a system of high human, social and ethical values, a high level of social, cultural and human awareness, and a strong sense of commitment, self-confidence, intelligence and independent thinking.

The history of human civilization is replete with examples of such individuals who were triggering agents of change and movement of history.

Contentment with the Familiar and Open Mindedness

Place of one's birth is not meant to be a prison. It is natural that the newly-born is open to the wider world surrounding him. Birth is the gate to be open to the world. Birth is the beginning of one's interaction. Man's openness to the world would be helped to be achieved with interaction and dialogue with it. This dialogue wouldn't take place unless one's talk and writing about himself and life are frank and devoid of hesitation and fear, expressing his true feeling. Intellectual dialogue and openness are achieved with seeing things as they are.

Self-contentment is feeling at home with the familiar. Self-contentment, whether individually or collectively, if it indicates lack of interest in things that are not included in what makes one contented, is a sort of impenetrability, because it means structurally and functionally lack of going beyond the boundary of the scope of that contentment. Contentment with the familiar is intellectual inertia. It paralyzes intellectual freedom and innovation. This type of self-contentment discourages dialogue and interaction and, hence, open-mindedness. It is indifferent to the existence of multiple intellectual and practical choices and alternatives.

Contentment with the familiar is lack of openness to the unfamiliar. Contentment with the self and with the familiar reflects indifference to unfamiliar possibilities and visions, and involves exclusion of what the self is not aware of, including the unfamiliar. It may be good to go beyond the limits of the familiar which accepts one reading of circumstances and developments and imposes its one reading on the layers of the people and chases other readings.

As contentment with the familiar impedes interaction and open-mindedness, it is intellectually restrictive. As moving within the circle of the familiar excludes exposure to the unfamiliar, this confinement to the familiar supports impenetrability and suppresses interest in the unfamiliar.

As it affirms and strengthens intellectual impenetrability, one needs, in order to be interactive and open-minded, to depart from contentment with the familiar. This contentment makes one prefer the familiar reading to other readings. Thus, this contentment is intellectually suppressive.

As contentment with the familiar weakens or paralyzes intellectual creativity and as it makes one unmindful of the existence of the multiplicity of intellectual alternatives, then one who seeks to be free from these effects needs to depart from contentment with the familiar. This can be achieved through intellectual interaction and open-mindedness. A person who is dissatisfied with one reading of events, developments and circumstances has the urge to experience more than one reading and does not want to view things and phenomena through the prism of his own familiar world; he feels the need to widen the boundaries of the familiar by crossing into the unfamiliar. Leaving the familiar is expression of the psychological emancipation and a leaning towards intellectual independence, an affirmation of the self and an indication of the leap of the self and vitality of the human race.

As being contented with the familiar is intellectual dependence on the propositions of this contentment, departure from contentment with the familiar is a manifestation of intellectual independence and a psychological breakthrough. People who confine their interpretation of their life's necessities to their familiar circle are highly likely to be people who do not know how to defend themselves. That is because people whose behavior reaches into the unfamiliar world are made aware of more options with which to express ideas that might sway peoples who are captive of their familiar world.

Emancipation from the familiar is self-affirmation, which is an indication of the existence of viable individual. People who do not affirm themselves, who dare not to do that, and do not know that fact are vulnerable people who are unable to face challenges, interior or exterior.

Related to contentment is silence. There are undisclosed things and unknown things or things about which there is silence. There are social and psychological situations in which social and intellectual progress cannot be achieved except with the discovery of the existence of such things. Because of fear of being exposed to criticism or persecution from influential actors in society, people usually refrain from the attempt to reveal the existence of hidden things or things about which there is silence.

Reading and Political-Cultural Projection

A characteristic of reading is that it is not possible to have congruence between reading and the text being read, as such a text is amenable to more than one reading. There is no abstract reading. Reading is not a mere echo of the text. Reading is one of the texts' many probabilities. In reading a text, a reader is not like a mirror, with no role except to reflect images, concepts and meanings, which the creator of the text wanted to express fully and literally. Text always admits of interpretation, and calls for reading in it what it has not been read.

Hence, reading of one text differs with each reading, and between one reader and the other. Reading even differs with the same reader according to his circumstances and social-cultural background. A reader may be seen as more than one reader. A reader may be seen as many readers as the number of different readings he has of a text.

Not infrequently, listeners or readers face difficulty in understanding text. The nature of the content of text is partially responsible for this difficulty. The difficulty is also attributable to other factors, such as the awareness or unawareness of the reader with which he faces the text. By facing that text with this awareness or unawareness, the reader erects actually a barrier with a certain effectiveness vis-à-vis the flow of the text's meaning to the recipient. Through this process, what can be called 'domestication" or taming of the text, or making it more acceptable or familiar, occurs. From this process results that the text is distanced from its original intended or desired content. Through this process, the content of the text is subjected, to a certain extent, to the understanding with that awareness, because this awareness has its reflections on the contents of the read writings. Moreover, awareness has its priorities with respect to the aspects of the intended contents that the awareness absorbs.

To read may positively interact with the read material. With that interaction, there would be a removal of the address of the one prescriptive, commanding, dominating and dictating meaning that no one has the ability and courage to study and discuss, to explain and criticize, and to have reservations on it.

Interactive, critical and conscious reading is a pillar of democratic and intellectual dialogue. In this reading, the text is not assumed to be containing full truth, but it would be the subject of examination and criticism. Through this conscious and critical reading, a reader enters unlimited intellectual horizons, for in this way of reading there would be no high authority that determines the meaning and the accuracy of the text. Critical and conscious reading involves taking a considerably liberated and new look at the text, the self, the people and the universe. With this reading, domination of the patriarchal thinking thus becomes restricted or removed.

A major defect of a considerable portion of human thought is logically and intellectually unjustified projection of concepts. Because of the human nature and of the social-psychological background, cultural-political projection takes place, namely, conversion of the analysis process to a process of converting matter which was intended to be analyzed and explained, to a process of recreating it. In cultural projection, where one projects himself on what he was saying that he was analyzing, what was said to be "object of analysis" loses its being an object, and becomes a product of active interactions of the personality of the one who carries out the projection. Thus, through this projection, the process of analysis and of explanation is suppressed by the process of subjective conversion.

One of the important factors which determines the extent of difference or extent of distance between one's analysis and conversion which he creates is the extent of his ability to create a distance between himself and what he is studying and analyzing, and the extent of his ability to separate between the self and the object. The longer is the distance, assuming that such a distance is there, the closer was the conversion to the process of analysis. Actually, separation between the subjective and objective aspects in the self is almost impossible.

A proof of the partiality of analysis is that one who studies something determines his starting point on the basis of his personality and background. It is described as a beginning from the viewpoint of a person. It may not deserve to be described that it is a starting point from the viewpoint of somebody else, of the historical context, of the proper perspective, or of the comprehension of outlook.

This is not the only 'beginning' for the student. During the process of this treatment, each decision made by him would be a 'beginning' also.

Through cultural-political projection, the personality of the person dealing with something swallows that thing. He does not see that thing far away from him, an object, or that there is a distance between him and the thing. For that person, the thing which is being dealt with is functional, performing the function of realizing the expectations of the treating person, affirming his biased perceptions and justifying the position taken towards the treated thing; thus, that person may become satisfied.

With this projection, the thing under treatment also becomes relative to the person doing the treatment. The history of the thing under treatment, its culture, civilization, beliefs, life and aspirations are judged from the perspective of the treating person. The person being treated may be an individual, a people, a nation, a continent, a culture, a mind, or any other entity; and the actor doing the treatment may also be an individual, a group, an army, a government, or something else. A large section of the Orientalists' writings about the Arab and Islamic past and present in various fields, for example, has been a process of cultural-political projection.

This way of projection of concepts has led and continues o lead to the commission of many and big intellectual and practical errors. This way leads to intellectual suppression, as generalizing of a concept by projecting it on other concepts means inattention to the intellectual being of each of these concepts, which means defacing and suppression of that entity through the imposition of the intellectual entity of the concept which is being projected on other entities that are subjected to the projection of that concept.

This projection means that dialogue is not held between concepts; it means impenetrability of the concept projected on the concepts subjected to projection, and it means intellectual dictation on them. With this projection, the concept is not open to other concepts, but its entity was expanded at the expense of the other concepts.

Social Change and Technology

The socio-cultural and intellectual development taking place in the world involves change, to variable extents, in the intellectual positions in various fields. This change may be represented in one's second thinking about some habits and practices to which one is used, or in one's leaving in his self a space in which he allows himself to be more neutral or less restrictive or bigot vis-à-vis some questions.

Social change and its pace are influenced by technological development. Social change is more likely to be faster where there is a greater degree of technological development.

Human beings, in any society, live according to their social values and norms, which limit and condition human behavior. These values have a say in their actions and reactions.

The behavior of technology lacks consideration for social values and norms. This lack accounts for social change. When technology, which is man-made, is in operation, its action or behavior is not socially or value-conditioned. When operation of a technological instrument is stopped through interference of a human agent, the instrument is made to stop.

There is precise, clear-cut, machine-like, exact behavior. This behavior is not susceptible to social values and conditions, including social norms and considerations, in the sense that once it was begun, it takes its course of action naturally, irrespective of any social condition. The precision and non-amenability of this behavior to social condition could not be compromised or controlled in its course of action. In this sense, this behavior is "blind." It is humanly controllable, in the sense that it could be stopped.

There is, on the other hand, social behavior, in the sense that it is value-laden, value-conditioned, value-controlled or value-driven. The difference between the exact behavior and the socially value-laden behavior varies from one society to another and from one time to another, following the level of social development of a given society in a given time.

The similarity or dissimilarity of value-laden behavior to exact behavior is related to the level of social development.

The type of relationship between the exact behavior and the socially value-laden behavior is indicative of the level or stage of social development. When the exact behavior is geared to, compromised in favor of, or subjected to the value-laden behavior in a given society, this is indicative of a low social development of that society. In a more developed society, the contrary happens, namely, the value-laden behavior is inferior or gives way to the exact behavior. The more a society is developed, the greater is the inferiority of the value-laden behavior to the exact behavior and vice versa.

Value-laden type of behavior is more commonly spread among illiterate, homogenous and traditional societies, with a stronger sense of group solidarity. In these societies relations are more personal, uncritical and traditional, the sacred prevails over the secular, where actions and relationships are more based on, determined by, and oriented towards the family and the clan, where organization is not based on professional differentiation, where particularistic and diffuse relationships predominate, where use of money and of markets is more limited, and where the clan affiliation has a predominant role as a controlling agent and as an agent which teaches, prepares and gives orientation.

More exact behavior is one which is more typical of societies where patterns of behavior differ from those characteristic of the above-mentioned societies. Exact behavior is more discernible in more modernized societies, where organization is more set along specialization and professionalism, where functions are more specific and less diffuse, where use of money and markets is more widespread, where clan roles are less significant, and where urbanization and industrialization is more advanced.

There are contexts or social environments in which these two kinds of behavior come into contact with each other. Since the one type of behavior is inherently on intrinsically not compromising, while the other type is socially conditioned, then when these two types of behavior come into contact with each other they conflict or collide with each other. This collision produces certain responses or reactions by the behaving (human and non-human) agents of the collision. As the exact behavior is a party in the collision, or as this behavior has helped produce it, the human agent in the collision who was performing a socially conditioned behavior would undergo a new type of experience, to which he was not used or accustomed before, one which would open the mind of the human agent to the fact that there are other types of behavior than that to which he was heretofore accustomed, or with which he was acquainted.

The type of the experience of the human agent is new because of the precision of the behavior of one of the two types of behavior involved in the collision. The precision of this behavior was unfamiliar, strange, novel or foreign to the human agent. Since the collision situation has an element of novelty, the responses by the human agent resulting from the collision situation should be new and different from the socially familiar responses.

Way of life and of handling matters, which defines culture, determines, to a far extent, history, past and legacy. Given the fact that peoples have various ways of living and of handling matters, peoples have different cultures.

There are cases in which change of social institutions is beneficial to people and society. In some cultures, of which are some aspects of Western societies, there is a strong tendency to paying attention to speed of change in social institutions which play important and vital social roles, and there are cultures, some of which are aspects of traditional culture, which pay less attention to the speed of change of those institutions which play those roles.

Nature of those social roles is a factor which determines the importance of the greater or lesser speed of change. This nature is determined by the characteristics of the values and main institutions of society and people.

Changes that are quickly sweeping the world are and will not bypass the developing peoples. These peoples should get themselves ready to accept loss of some customs and traditions and to change the way they deal with matters and things, because, among other things, the idea of loss is inherent in change.

Imposition by an actor, guided by its value and institutional background, of its conception of the priority of speed of change of its basic values and institutions on another society or people involves defacement and suppression in the intellectual field. In view of the fact that institutions and values differ from one culture to the other, the speed of change of institutions may not be suitable to another society at a certain time.

There are people, probably mainly in the developing countries, who attach a special subjective and objective importance to their history. In the Arab life, history plays a much more important role than that played by history in the lives of some other peoples, in making up the state, society and family, and in terms of the preservation of their values and cultural space. Imposition by foreign actors on the less developed countries the habit of change with excessive rate of speed and of their way of hurriedly dealing with the place and significance of history is a form of suppression of the cultural institutions which have the orientation of keeping of those contents and their strengthening in their life currently and in the future.

Even if objective need requires introduction of change in the view of the place of history in the life of the Arabs, and even if Arabs feel that it is necessary to make some reduction in the attention to the role of history in their lives, personality and institutions, that need may not reach the extent of make excessive change in the attention paid to the significance of history.

Amid Western societies some voices are heard that change with excessive speed is a welcome development. Experience during over two centuries, however, shows that the idea of excess in the speed of change is an excuse used by those to justify the attempt to weaken or deface non-Western cultures, and to justify the attempt to spread and solidify Western cultural influence.

With excessive speed of change, targeted objectives of change might be passed. Instead of achieving the objective of change, an impact other than the targeted impact might occur. With excessive speed of change, which is what we witness in some aspects of Western life, such change goes beyond the desired structural boundaries. Intellectual structures which are cut off from the context of the envisaged objective do not lead to the achievement of the objective. Social disintegration, intellectual chaos, spiritual loss, de-humanization and others may result from excessive speed of change.

Excessive speed of change makes the period of man's relation to things and to both the social and natural environments which are around him of short duration. This excess makes man lose sense of significant durability of his relation to what is around him, between human creatures, and between man and his past and his heritage. In the shadow of the culture of excessive rate of speed of change, child is quickly inculcated that home is a mere mechanism for processing: with this mechanism people enter and exit with higher rate of speed.

Given the fact that developing societies are passing through national, political and cultural development, it is reasonable that cultural and spiritual values drawn from the developing peoples' past would have a greater importance in their lives during developmental. With maintaining the link of history to the peoples facing various foreign influences and challenges, some compensation for the values lost by such peoples because of the excessive change takes place. However, imposition by certain foreign actors of various types of values and behavior on those peoples makes a great contribution to establishing the value and belief orientation of these peoples on the long term. With the existence of space which allows a person to be more neutral, it becomes easier for such actors to make such imposition more effective. That is what we are seeing taking place in the third world. That this is taking place involves intellectual and value suppression, as with foreign actors determining the intellectual and value orientation of the developing countries in the state of their development, there is suppression of emergence of other tendencies that would have emerged had it not been for the intervention of foreign actors, and it is likely that such suppressed tendencies would have included more original intellectual contents being inspired by the intellectual, scientific and civilization heritage of the developing countries.

Evasion of Frank Discussion and Intellectual Suppression

As ambiguity of treatment of matters hides known and unknown of their aspects, such ambiguity involves intellectual suppression. As ambiguity may be intentional or unintentional, intellectual defacement may be intentional or unintentional. Ambiguity of treatment may have the effect of encroachment, because of obscuring some aspects of matters, on the knowledge of aspects whose treatment was ambiguous. Ambiguity of treatment may be a means of evading the direct and frank treatment of such matters. More often than not, one, in writing or speech, may not treat a subject frankly and directly, because of his fear of being subjected to criticism and even a sort of punishment for his thought or his way of dealing with the subject.

Interaction, leading to open mindedness, wouldn't be achieved unless one's speech and writings about himself and life are frank and free from hesitation and fear, expressing his real feeling and emotion. Dialogue, interaction and open-mindedness are not achieved through hypocrisy, ambiguity, falsehood and masking one's true feelings. What contributes to the achievement of open mindedness is seeing things as they are.

Evasion of frank discussion of issues has also contributed to intellectual impenetrability. Evasion of placing issues on the table for discussion is encroachment on their eligibility to be discussed. A considerable number of writers in all countries—and, it seems, particularly in the developing countries—evade certain issues involving the relation between science and religion, the independence of science, the legal status of women, and political and social tyranny.

This evasion partially is out of fear of angering influential people at the official and unofficial levels and also the masses, because objective and rational treatment of such subjects might impinge on the feelings of people. By making thinking more impenetrable, evasion of frank discussion adversely affects intellectual and social interaction. Evasion of mention of ideas involves suppression of such ideas.

Climate of official and unofficial intellectual suppression leads to negative influence on the various aspects of discussion. One of these aspects is the choice of the subject of discussion. There are subjects that are more relevant to issues of politics, policy, government, authority and continued direction and control of the reins of power. These are subjects for which results and conclusions of discussion and research are more relevant.

It is highly likely that people in charge of authority are not interested, because, among other reasons, of their interest to continue and promote their authority, in the conduct of research which can reach conclusions and facts which would lead to the weakening of their status. Therefore, out of fear from upsetting those who are in power in many countries around the world, these researchers turn away from conduct of research into subjects which, with their results and conclusions, have a stronger relevance to the issues of the exercise of authority.

Questions that are discussed are interrelated. In order to achieve a comprehensive treatment of a particular case, the approach of treatment should be all-embracing, dealing with all the issues that factor in the emergence of the examined phenomenon. A phenomenon would not be adequately studied if the discussion covers non-controversial questions and does not cover the controversial questions.

Tone of conclusions of studies is another aspect on which the climate of official and unofficial authoritarian suppression has a very negative effect. In spite of the fact that the objective of study is to reach conclusions, these conclusion differ one from the other in terms of their strong or light tone. Through taking refuge in the use of softened or strong tone of conclusions a researcher can take into account consideration, such as—and primarily—his fear of governmental suppression, should these conclusions be critical of the authority's practices, thus leading to encroachment on the knowledge of the lived reality.

One of the defects of various cultures is resignation to political, economic and historical statements without having them studied adequately. Submission to such statements is tantamount to suppression of aspects of such a statement that have not been dealt with adequately. An adequate treatment of such aspects would have caused change in the developing peoples' views of the conclusions which were arrived at through the inadequate study.

Disproportion in Attribution of Responsibility

A flaw in the way of thinking in a considerable portion of written or spoken statements is not to specify the various and varying share of responsibility of various factors, political, economic, historical, psychological and cultural, for the development and explanation of social phenomena. This type of statement is deficient when it comes to the treatment of such phenomena. Given the lack of a complete knowledge of the relative weight of factors in the emergence of a certain phenomenon, sometimes to attribute a precise role in the emergence of a phenomenon involves a kind of intellectual suppression. This suppression is embodied in the over-emphasis on the part of some students of society, without sufficient evidence, of a certain factor in determining the relative strength of factors in bringing about the phenomenon.

In the attribution of the same share of responsibility to factors, there is a dichotomous and suppressive thought, as this way of treatment does not conceive of responsibility for a phenomenon as being a result of varying factors that, in their responsibility, are placed on a spectrum ranging from the smallest to the largest share of responsibility.

For example, writers have mentioned and continue to mention reasons or factors for Third World underdevelopment. These factors are known. May be it is appropriate to mention them here. The reasons are historical, cultural, economic, psychological, political, structural, internal and external. To go into a little detail, these factors include belief in superstition, domination of illusions, romantic outlook, despotic political and social legacy, marginalization of the status of women, intellectual inertia and laxity, indifference, sectarianism, tribalism, parochial outlook, foreign economic and political influence.

It seems obvious that these and other factors are responsible for the current miserable conditions in the developing, and even the developed, countries. What is conspicuous in the treatment of such factors is lack of specificity of the share of responsibility of each factor for these conditions.

This lack of specification has negative effects on the treatment of many of these ills. A more general statement of factors makes treatment more general, thus preventing more specific remedial prescription for particular cases.

Additionally, the shares of responsibility allocated by observers to mistaken actions are not equal. Mistakes have been made and continue to be made in many fields: In the understanding of the political, economic, cultural and psychological reality of oneself and of others, in the understanding of one's history, and in the way of dealing with the self and with others; and additionally, in the way states formulate their own regional and international policies, in the way developmental policies are implemented, and in the way decision-makers set their order of priorities. For example, what might be correct to describe as Western ethnocentrism has been a major factor in preventing Western peoples from better knowing and understanding non-Western peoples. Local, parochial or interest groups in the West have succeeded in erecting a barrier between the West and other peoples. There is a lot of witch-hunting in a number of Western countries.

Ideology and Criticism

One meaning of progress is the adoption of the concept of the continuous need to discover what has not yet been discovered of the emerging and changing phenomena, of the human beings' life, facts of self, society, state, nature and cosmos, and of the people's entrance to psychological and mental condition that makes them questioning and critical always, a matter which would lead to the emergence of continuously renewing thought.

Adoption of critical approach requires continuous treatment of issues that are not necessarily under consideration. To continue treatment of such issues is better than not to have them treated. Criticism of phenomena and things that are likely to be defective or flawed is better than not to have them criticized. Analysis of reality from its all of its aspects, its understanding and study of its truth, and attempt to make reference to alternatives are better than not to do that. It is of the utmost importance that this approach deals with the political situation as this situation is the most influential one. Through exercise of the critical approach it becomes easier for the human being to discover points of weakness and of strength. Through such an approach, spontaneity is reduced, study increases in importance, and substance is given more attention.

Intellectual interaction, which occurs through exercise of critical approach, helps to achieve intellectual open mindedness, as through such interaction and open mindedness it becomes possible to know alternatives.

Being a useful method in the acquisition of knowledge, criticism does not and should not sympathize with any ideology or writing, as such sympathy vitiates its function. To place conduct of criticism under the mastery of ideological drive vitiates the process of criticism. When criticism is exercised, this criticism is general, including written or verbal statements, irrespective of those who made them. When it is impossible to separate the sympathizer's position from the critique's position, then what is taking place is not just criticism, and the context is not just a critical context.

The concept of uncontestable ideas occupies only a small space in the questioning and critical thought. Critical thought is in contrast with the concept of uncontestable ideas. Critical thought naturally subjects each phenomenon to criticism, investigation, verification and examination. Acceptance of uncontestable ideas means the yielding of the critical thought; it is negation of critical thought. Adoption of the approach of critical thought means rejection of the concept of uncontestable ideas. Acceptance of uncontestable ideas means weakening of intellectual activity, exclusion or elimination. Progress cannot be achieved with the espousal of uncontestable ideas. Uncontestable ideas are perhaps contented with an amount of truths, whereas the many truths in the cosmos would only be discovered with critical thought.

A factor that prevents the mind from innovation and from objective and direct treatment of subjects has been the fear that to thought is mistakenly attributed heresy in religion. Developments of life at the present time require the coming up with new ideas that respond to such developments. There are fields and developments which require application of new thought without having such thought described as heretical. Thinkers, however, are fearful that the concept of heresy is attributed to their thought. Hence, they have no courage to come up with a new thought. There is a need for the concept of heresy, to be sufficiently and adequately defined and clarified as much as possible so that people interested in matters of thought would know matters of life where the concept of heresy does not apply.

A tendency on the part of a generation of the intelligentsia to disagree with preceding cultural generations or a coming cultural generation slows down or weakens cultural and intellectual development. It can be said that products of a certain cultural generation include useful and constructive ideas, regardless of the intellectual orientation of any intellectual-cultural generation. By disagreeing with preceding or coming cultural generations, no much room is left for the emerging generation to benefit from certain constructive ideas. Achievement by individuals from previous generations of intellectual, artistic, literary and philosophical creativity obviously does not mean end of the process of creativity. As a matter of fact, the process of educational-intellectual building on what has been achieved would create a space in which members of a new generation can make their creativity in the fields of thought, art, and literature. As creativity includes experimentation, difference, intellectual emancipation, for an intellectual generation to disagree with, or to fight, another intellectual generation is tantamount to fighting the process of creativity.

Excess of Commendation
and Intellectual Restriction

A widespread phenomenon that does not help in reaching truth or what is taken as truth is that of exaggeration or excess of praise or commendation.

An outstanding, distinguished or achieving individual, for instance, a commander, writer, thinker, literary figure or philosopher, might be welcomed or received in an exaggerated manner by peoples who have different convictions.

Both excessive praise and hypocrisy are taken as a means to people's protection in social and political environments that threaten their lives or as a means to establish closer ties with influential groups, including governmental and non-governmental authorities or to promote their interests in forms such as obtaining money and filling post vacancies.

The phenomenon of the excess of commendation means relaxing of the criterion of merit or disregard of such a criterion. Many times, expressions of commendation of a certain person—be it and individual or entity—are used to a far-reaching extent, to an extent to which it is impossible to add to this commendation. In such cases, it is sweeping and comprehensive without reservation. Thus, it is impossible to depict another person who is superior to the first praised person with a description stronger than that used to depict the first person, in spite of the fact that the other person, because of his superior talents, qualification and achievements, deserves that depiction.

Given the fact that the human being lacks in perfection, commendation due to excellence or distinction in one field should not deny critics the right to exercise criticism.

Moreover, his distinction in one kind of creativity should not mean that his creative products should be exempt from criticism in other fields. To commend a person for all of his contributions because of his excellence in only one field is very costly intellectually as in this approach inheres gross intellectual limitation; it limits the intellectual freedom and poses a challenge of exploring and knowing reality.

This intellectual tendency to intellectual dichotomous division indicates inadequate intellectual development. This approach indicates that that developed has not crossed this simplistic dichotomous division; it impedes adequate intellectual development and generation of more developed and complex thought.

Exaggerated welcome might have negative results. For instance, excess in welcome of philosopher might make him like a prisoner, and he might have the feeling that he needs to be freed from such a prison.

With this excessive welcome an individual might feel that people do not understand him or do not know his thought, and that people welcome him because they have not fathomed his thought. He might be thinking that have they known his thought they might have not well received him. They respect him on the basis of their conception of his thought, while that conception does not necessarily match with his thought. He might know that a gap does exist between his thought and peoples' conception of his thought. He might not want this state of affairs.

It is notably difficult for some writers or thinkers, for instance, to make people know them well. Sometimes, a thinker's thought is less fragmented and more coherent from thought of certain segments of society. Belonging to a certain kind of speech, which characterizes many people, means fragmentation of thought; it means a partial and fragmented thought. The source of welcome or respect by people with divergent discourses of speech is that these people were able to find in their discourses room for what they conceive of as the thinker's thought. Thus, accommodation of his thought in their discourses is a fragmentation of his thought and a distortion and lack of its understanding.

This is realized by thinkers. For them, alignment with a certain discourse of speech might be an opposition to their thought and restriction to it. It is but natural that thinkers do not tolerate that relations between them and others are on the basis of their mistaken conception of his thought. Relations on such basis restrict thinkers' freedom which is very valued by them.

Of relevance in this context is excessive courtesy. Courtesy has some relation to expression of respect. Excessive courtesy dominates the behavior of some people, in particular among the developing peoples. It has a dangerous drawback, because it comes at the expense of acquisition of knowledge and of behavioral firmness. It prevents, to a considerable degree, behavior which is made necessary by interests and exploration, whereas conduct of proper social relations requires frankness, firmness, objectivity and straightforwardness, all of which are not compatible with excessive courtesy.

Means to Weaken Dichotomy

Important means that would weaken intellectual extremism and intellectual dichotomy is availability of a group of factors acting simultaneously. These means include reduction of illiteracy rate, acquisition of professional literacy, raising of the educational level, raise of level of living, development of the concept of citizenship, protection of human rights, de-patriarchialization of social, political and economic life, gender equality in proper fields, and spread of a greater amount of democratization of the social and political life. This democratization involves recognition of intellectual pluralism, which is not compatible with intellectual exclusion and suppression. Such pluralism would be strengthened by democratic institutions such as parliaments, parties, and freedom of expression.

Such factors can be achieved gradually and in simultaneous and consecutive times, as undertaking of unsynchronized actions would impair their effectiveness. Each factor may individually have an effect in the direction of weakening such dichotomy, but the social, cultural, political and psychological environment can considerably paralyze the effect of such individual factor; it is much more difficult for such an environment to paralyze the effect of the above-mentioned factors when combined.

What would further weaken intellectual suppression is the emergence of civil society comprising various bodies, such as cultural, political intellectual, literary and sports associations, philanthropic and voluntary societies, and productive and industrial labor unions and organizations. That is because civil society provides intellectual multilateralism and intellectual currents through making possible exchange of ideas and exercise of dialogue in the crystallization of ideas and positions. In the shadow of civil society, each intellectual current is allowed to have its followers, and followers of other currents are not allowed to impose their visions on the followers of other currents. The functions of democratic institutions and institutions of modern society include curbing of intellectual oppression which is exercised by governmental and non-governmental authorities which have adopted the approach of uniform line of thinking regardless of the changing circumstances.

Peoples won't achieve progress nor would they enjoy the adequate means of self-defense without the recognition of unacceptability of dichotomy, and of the relativity of things and the soundness of intellectual emancipation, and without their managing their life accordingly.

A Holistic Approach to Development and Underdevelopment

The verb 'develop' is not used as intransitive, but as transitive. Development is taken to mean an intended change to achieve certain goals in the familiar fields, such as cultural, political, economic factors and others.

One of the defects of various cultures, which hinders or slows down development, is resignation to political, economic and historical statements without having them studied adequately. Submission to such statements is tantamount to suppression of aspects of such a statement that have not been dealt with adequately. An adequate treatment of such aspects would have caused change in the developing peoples' views of the conclusions which were arrived at through the inadequate study.

An additional factor that hinders or slows down the achievement of an intended change is the lack of tools needed to bring about such change. These tools include, but not limited to, political will, expertise, finance and organization.

One more factor is the different definitions of concepts, such as change, development and intention. For example, one may regard change as a change in certain circumstances, ignoring his own or her own change as relevant for the change in those circumstances. Because of dynamic interaction, change in a person is relevant for change in a circumstance.

One additional factor is an inadequate awareness of the influence of unrecognized, latent or unseen factors on the recognized factors. This influence may lead to undoing or vitiating, partially or fully, change achieved through the recognized factors. For example, a change, such as winning of political independence, may be vitiated by a reckless or a dictatorial leader.

Moreover, people differ in their perception of the realization of concepts. Some may regard as realization a partial implementation or accommodation of a certain factor or concept. This may hinder change, as such insufficient implementation may be incapable to withstand, or cope with, other factors, recognized or unrecognized, that have a strong impact on the concepts which were only partially realized. For example, establishment of universities which do follow a traditional method of imparting information cannot cope with the ignored need to instill in students the capacity of independent and interactive thinking.

Another factor which exists in reality is the competing factors which have contradictory effects on intended change. An example may be the case where a factor for change, for example a higher level of living as a result of a higher rate of school and college enrolment contradicts with a higher birth rate resulting from the same factor.

A factor which may prevent or slow down intended change is the political one. A political factor is defined as the strong motivation on the part of a person to acquire the ability to exercise influence in order to achieve certain goals. This motivation to acquire influence is found in the governmental and non-governmental, and official and unofficial, domains. People generally enjoy exertion of influence and power. A political person would be less than cooperative in the achievement of change should he or she view such change as compromising his/her influence, power or authority.

Implications of ethical orientation are an important factor in causing change. Tools which can cause change, such as finance, technology, science, expertise, knowledge and organization, are not adequate in themselves to cause such change. To a considerable degree, such tools are value-free or value-neutral. They lend themselves to programs, plans, intentions or agendas, regardless of the ethical orientation of such plans and intentions. Such ethical orientation affects the way tools for the cause of change are used; such orientation has a strong say in the dedication or lack of it to the intended change and in the way the political factor is addressed. A dictator is unlikely to support change for democracy.

Development is an integrated process. As the process is integrated, it cannot occur in an area while it is absent in other relevant areas. Agricultural progress is not achieved without achievement of a measure of industrial progress, and the progress in this field cannot be achieved without achievement of a measure of economic progress; an economic progress cannot be achieved without an advanced mentality; mental progress cannot be achieved without application of an advanced teaching and educational system. This system is not achieved without achievement of a measure of good management and organization. These facets of progress—which involve development—cannot be achieved without allowing of opportunity for intellectual creativity which is psychological-mental process. By the same token, intellectual creativity cannot be achieved without an appreciable measure of intellectual, psychological and political freedom. This lack of consideration means that a person not taking integration into account is imposing his mistaken thought on how to achieve the process of progress.

In order to be able to achieve socio-political and cultural development, a comprehensive or holistic approach needs to be adopted. In human society, where factors of development or counteracting factors of stagnation and underdevelopment may exist, to use only a part of the factors of development would not yield the desired results. For whatever achievement the limited factors of progress can accomplish would be rendered insignificant or vitiated by the factors that work in the direction of the *status quo*.

Moreover, at the early stages of a progress, the working of factors of advancement would still be more effective. In the passage of time, however, facing and confronting factors of stagnation, factors of change and development are likely to lose momentum.

Because of the enormity and complexity of the cultural-political advancement, an approach involving all the factors involved should be adopted. These factors include, but are not limited to, spread of learning, professionalism, democracy, giving deserved weight to science and allowance for the emergence of civil organizations. With taking into account of all of the factors which work for development under certain value system, development would be promoted. With taking into account of only some of these factors would weaken their sought effect, as there would still be some fields that are not covered by the left-out factors. These uncovered fields would vitiate the good effects of the factors that were taken into account.

Different roads were proposed as leading to the desired change, to revival, awakening and development. Modernization, secularism, socialism, adherence to religious prescriptions, criticism and science are examples of these perceived roads. I think that such concepts, though different one from the other, can co-exist in a certain social setting; they have the ability to develop, in a certain social setting, certain relations of co-existence and adjustment intellectually and practically. This co-existence would be easier to achieve for peoples of civilizations, who have creative imagination and a legacy of tolerance and diversity.

Obviously, of relevance is to go into the reasons for underdevelopment. One reason for underdevelopment is misconception of religion. Priorities of religious law are not observed.

Another reason is despotism and tyranny by the rulers. Solution lies in democratization. Through it, people return to the theater of history.

To achieve development, what is also needed is active critical approach, which requires active critical awareness. With this awareness, other factors would be taken account of.

With this awareness, the role of ideology and romantic thinking would be reduced. To achieve development, thought should not be jailed in romantic and unrealistic thinking. With a critical mind, mind would reach humanistic and embracing outlook. With a critical approach, a mind can recognize other minds and minds can begin an era of a genuine dialogue. Cultures, then can meet on a common and shared ground.

Both development and underdevelopment are a cultural, psychological and mental condition, as well as a material and technological condition. Because of that, development can only be achieved gradually and underdevelopment can only be eliminated gradually. Given the complexity of the condition of underdevelopment, it is impossible to have it removed at once. In order to expedite the elimination of underdevelopment, it is necessary to promote the ideas of intellectual and political freedom, innovation and creativity; rule of law; and democracy.

A Select Bibliography

Peter Bachrach and Morton S. Baratz, <u>Power and Poverty: Theory and Practice.</u> Vol. 197 (Oxford: Oxford University Press, 1970).

T. B. Bottomore, <u>Elites and Society</u> (Baltimore: Penguin Books, 1966).

Edward McNall Burns and others, eds., <u>World Civilizations: Their History and the Culture</u> (New York: Norton, 1986).

William H. Dray, ed., <u>Philosophical Analysis and History</u> (New York: Harper & Row, 1966).

Andrew Effrat, ed., <u>Perspectives in Political Sociology</u> (New York: Bobbs-Merrill, 1972).

Patrick Hossay, <u>Unsustainable; a Primer for Global Environmental and Social Justice</u> (London: Zed Books, 2006).

Ibn Khaldun, <u>The Muqaddimah; an Introduction to History.</u> Translated from the Arabic by Franz Rosenthal; edited and abridged by N. J. Dawood (Princeton: Bollingen Series, 1969).

Evelyn Fox Keller, "Feminism and Science," in <u>The Philosophy of Science</u>, ed. by Richard Boyd, Philip Gasper and J.D. Trout (Cambridge, MA: MIT Press, 1991).

Harold R. Kerbo, <u>Social Stratification and Inequality</u> (New York: McGraw-Hill, 2008).

Harold D. Lasswell, <u>Politics: Who Gets What, When, How </u>(New York: Meridian Books, 1958).

Jeff Manza and Clem Brooks, <u>Social Cleavages and Political Change: Voter Alignments and U.S. Party Coalitions</u> (Oxford: Oxford University Press, 1999).

C. Wright Mills, <u>The Power Elite</u> (London: Oxford University Press, 1956).

Nagel, "The Value-Oriented Bias of Social Inquiry," in <u>Readings in the Philosophy of the Social Sciences</u>, ed. by May Brodbeck (London: Macmillan, 1969).

Taysir Nashif, <u>Society, Intellectuals and Cultural Change in the Developing Countries</u> (New York: iUniverse, 2006).

Martin O'Brien, Sue Penna and Colin Hay, eds., <u>Theorizing Modernity: Reflexivity, Environment and Identity in Giddens' Social Theory</u> (London: Longman Group, 1999).

Robert D. Putnam, <u>The Comparative Study of Political Elites</u> (NJ: Prentice-Hall, 1976).

Matilda White Riley and Edward E. Nelson, <u>Sociological Observation</u> (New York: Basic Books, 1974).

L. G. Seligman, "Political Recruitment and Party Structure: A Case Study," <u>American Political Science Review</u>, 55, 1961.

Hisham Sharabi, <u>Arab Intellectuals and the West: the Formative Years, 1875-1914</u> (Baltimore: The Johns Hopkins Press, 1970).

United Nations Development Program (UNDP). <u>Human Development Report 2001</u> (Geneva, United Nations, 2001).

Robin M. Williams, Jr., "Individual and Group Values," in <u>Readings in Sociology</u>. Fourth ed. by Edgar A. Schuler and others (New York: Crowell, 1972).

Edward O. Wilson, <u>The Diversity of Life</u> (New York: W.W. Norton, 1992).